William Babcock Weeden, William Babcock Weeden

The Morality of Prohibitory Liquor Laws

William Babcock Weeden, William Babcock Weeden

The Morality of Prohibitory Liquor Laws

ISBN/EAN: 9783743417755

Manufactured in Europe, USA, Canada, Australia, Japa

Cover: Foto ©Suzi / pixelio.de

Manufactured and distributed by brebook publishing software (www.brebook.com)

William Babcock Weeden, William Babcock Weeden

The Morality of Prohibitory Liquor Laws

"The justest laws are the truest." — EPICTETUS.

"Civil liberty is the not being restrained by any law, but which conduces in a greater degree to the public welfare." — PALEY.

"Good and stable government is simply or nearly impossible, unless the fundamentals of political science be known by the bulk of the people." — HOBBES.

THE MORALITY

OF

PROHIBITORY LIQUOR LAWS.

An Essay.

BY

WILLIAM B. WEEDEN.

BOSTON:

ROBERTS BROTHERS.

1875.

Cambridge:
Press of John Wilson & Son.

PREFACE.

THE matter of these pages was suggested in a paper read to the Unitarian National Conference at Saratoga. A prominent politician, a sincere and eminent advocate of prohibition, said to the writer directly, " This is an old story of yours; it is worn threadbare." Inasmuch as several able members of that capable association, men versed in the literature of law and social science, had said that the argument, whatever its merits, was novel and original, the remark of the politician set the writer into a train of thinking. The able men knew more of the philosophy of law, but the politician represented more people. It is perhaps this stolid indifference among persons holding high public trusts to the causes, the underlying principles, and the results of their own action, which has led the writer to develop his theme and bring it before the whole public. The subject is so important in all its bearings, that any sincere study of it can do no harm, and must be welcomed by all thoughtful persons.

The writer believes that the whole fabric of our legal and political action has been strained and injured by the institution and administration of these liquor laws. He believes that one of the first and most important steps in the much talked about reform of civil government must be, to turn the humane temperance impulse away from its abnormal action in law and in the state, and to give it natural play in the ethical improvement of the individual man and of society. If these pages contain any facts, or show any reasons which may help to forward this issue, his labor has not been in vain.

W. B. W.

PROVIDENCE, R.I., January, 1875.

CONTENTS.

	PAGE
INTRODUCTORY	9
TEMPERANCE AND ABSTINENCE	31
THE WORKING OF PROHIBITION	56
THE GROUNDS OF PROHIBITION	99
PROHIBITION AND REGULATION	121
ANOTHER SYSTEM	158
IMMORAL LAW-MAKING	179

INTRODUCTORY.

THIS is not an argument for or against total abstinence. The movement for temperance reform within the present century has divided the American people into three classes: those who refuse, those who use, and those who abuse liquors; or, to characterize them in the briefest terms, abstinents, temperates, and intemperates. The distinction between abstinence and temperance is pure matter of fact, which the words embody in themselves. Temperance and intemperance in the use of liquors are as old as the vine itself. Americans, with their natural love of association and organized action, formed societies rather more than fifty years ago to withstand intemperance.

"As soon as several of the inhabitants of the United States have taken up an opinion or a feeling
1*

which they wish to promote in the world, they look out for mutual assistance; and as soon as they have found each other out, they combine. From that moment they are no longer isolated men, but a power seen from afar, whose actions serve for an example, and whose language is listened to. The first time I heard in the United States that a hundred thousand men had bound themselves publicly to abstain from spirituous liquors, it appeared to me more like a joke than a serious engagement; and I did not at once perceive why these temperate citizens could not content themselves with drinking water by their own firesides. I at last understood that these hundred thousand Americans, alarmed by the progress of drunkenness around them, had made up their minds to patronize temperance. They acted just in the same way as a man of high rank who should dress very plainly, in order to inspire the humbler orders with a contempt of luxury."— *Democracy in America.* By De Tocqueville. Bowen's Trans. Vol. ii. 133.

This power of association is natural and healthful in our country. As the reform progressed, the term " temperance," together with the idea of temperance, as it is applied to all other appetites, fell into abeyance. Total ab-

'stinence and teetotalism became the watch-words of the reformers.

This distinction between temperance and abstinence is now well ingrained in mature individuals. The writer accepts this social fact as he finds it, and proposes no direct argument on this issue. He would not touch it indirectly, if the main question did not sometimes demand it. The enthusiasm of the abstinents, in its personal and legitimate expression, is not to be trifled with, nor even argued with. It is a noble passion, ever elevating, though sometimes narrowing the man, and is entitled to respect and affectionate regard from all of us. The man or woman who deliberately abandons liquors is generally moved from the depths of the soul. Those who have suffered, not in themselves, but in the wasted lives of their friends, cherish a passion for abstinence, which is beyond and above criticism. We say again, that we honor this emotion as one of the grand forces of humanity.

The moral influence of abstinents should likewise have the fullest play. The personal power of one who refuses an indulgence is the strongest motive to influence the self-indulgent. Society should favor this power of the individual by every means possible.

It is the civic attitude — using this term in the lack of a better — of the abstinents which the writer would call into the discussion. We would ask all abstinents to consider carefully their bearing toward society in its forms of law and civil government.

By as much as we exalt and dignify the moral power of the abstinents, by so much do we dread its waste or misuse in the struggle to maintain laws faulty in conception, impossible in execution. We do not expect to convince the old teetotal war-horses, who started in youth determined to force law into total abstinence. These men, made morbid by their horror of drink and by years of contest with reckless rum-sellers, have lost the sense of justice which keeps freedom alive. An old mechanic, whose thumb is made callous by long use of his tool, no longer guides it by the quick and supple sense which controlled it in his youth ; he moves it by an old instinct; so these teetotalers, blunted in the struggle, fail to find tyranny in any law against rum, or moral perversion in any legal wrong which aims at right. A younger generation is coming forward, who see the fearful strain upon law which our national life-struggle and our material prosperity have brought upon us. We would ask of them to consider from their own point of view their attitude toward law, — not any particular statute, but those great principles of government which hold society together.

The civic attitude of the abstinents may be briefly stated thus. Liquor is a poison: always dangerous, it is positively bad for healthy people. To use it is to incur a fearful risk for ourselves, to injure others, to injure the state ; let us stop the use of it. We are aware that not all abstinents claim that liquor is a poison, but this is the attitude of the party as a whole. Society in mass never would say outright that liquor was a poison, and was always bad. Its course was curiously inconsistent. Thirty to forty years ago New England was greatly shaken by the total abstinence movement. The imagination of the people was powerfully moved, and their moral sense was quickened into new action. Public sentiment was so strong that abstinence became common and temperance almost universal in the villages. In cities the current was in the same direction, though less decided, and the intemperate drinkers became few. The reformers then cherished the hope that a new generation, educated under the abstinence principle, would further strengthen public sentiment; that the use of liquors would almost or quite cease among decent people; and that the whole moral force of the better disposed elements of society would restrain the few who could not control their passions, or the intemperates.

This was too slow a process for the more ardent of the abstinents. They determined to

turn the force already acquired into a new chan-
nel, and to bring the whole power of society,
through the administration of law, to bear on
the use of liquors. This system culminated in
the Maine Law, so called, which, in its various
forms of prohibition and execution by state con-
stabularies, has dragged its way through legislatures and courts for more than twenty years.

How were these laws made, and how administered? The abstinents in New England,
where these laws have developed most strongly,
were never a majority.[1] The main body of the

[1] We seldom realize how small a number of voters actually believe in prohibitory law. We cite from the "New York
Evening Post": —

"One of the points in political discussion seems to have been
pretty well settled by the recent elections; namely, that the
people do not approve of sumptuary laws, and that no party
of any consequence can be organized upon the policy of prohibiting instead of regulating the sale of intoxicating liquors. We
have not yet the full returns of the vote in this State, but from
the indications we judge that the prohibitory vote amounted
to only a few thousands, although the prohibitory candidate
for governor, Mr. Myron H. Clark, was formerly an influential
politician and once held the governor's office. In Massachusetts Mr. Talbot was defeated, although the rest of the Republican State ticket received substantial majorities of the popular
vote, because he is an uncompromising prohibitionist, and
would have stood in the way of modifying the present prohib-

people were temperates, and we mean to include in this class every one who uses and does not abuse liquors, whether by the teaspoonful or by the glass. After the first excitement of the Washingtonian reform was over, the moderate men would not admit in fact that the use of liquors was always bad. They would not even submit to strict medical rule. In conduct each man should be his own physician, and prescribe when the little for the stomach's sake was necessary. This was a freeman's privilege, and they would keep it. We are not speaking of social drinkers nor tippling convalescents, but of the great body of sober, discreet citizens, who were neither abstinents nor intemperates. Their votes have decided all the prohibitory issues. These men seemed to move in a sort of intellectual stupor, brought on by the moral enthusiasm of the abstinents and their own contemplation

itory law. In Ohio, with the aid of the women's temperance crusade, the prohibitory vote was less than ten thousand. And, last and least of the instances we now recall, in Illinois, where the total vote for State officers was more than three hundred thousand, the highest vote for a candidate of the prohibitionists was 1,446, or less than half of one per cent."

of the horrors of intemperance. Any thing to stop traffic in the accursed stuff, the abstinents cried out. Law after law was enacted in different States; the temperates blindly voting whatever was wanted. Lawyers shook their heads, and physicians doubted, but the current moved on. Possibly the legal outlet afforded a relief from the excitement of the moral impulse under which the community labored. To put one moral reform under control of government and get it out of the daily duty of the individual, seemed a gain to some short-sighted persons. Nevertheless, steady-minded people could not vote it a poison. The statutes were all arranged with contrivances to allow the use under one and another sort of fiction. The contrivances and evasions passed into ordinary customs, while the statutes were constantly growing more stringent technically.

The abstinents, in their civic attitude, as we term it, took nearly the same ground which of old the church held in its administration of theology through its relation with the state. It

B

was evil to hold a wrong opinion in theology, a heresy; it injured the holder, it injured his neighbor, injured the state. It seemed good to authority in the olden time to restrain, imprison, even to kill the heretic. Modern liberty would say, the bad opinion, the heresy, will work itself out sooner if let alone by authority. We are aware some abstinents would say they mean to restrain the individual not in his own rights of liberty, but in his power to injure others, when they make a prohibitory statute. We hope to show farther on, that they must begin by tyranny over the individual, and we assume that position now. No teetotaler ever viewed the drunkard or the drinking corruption with greater horror than Loyola and Torquemada saw the heretic and the sinful results of heresy. To them, any use of power any force which we call tyranny, was better than the sufferance of wrong belief, which would carry souls to hell. It is only lately that civil government has abandoned that control over the opinions of the individual. The principle was not confined to any form of government; it belonged to human society, and dwelt alike in theocracy, papacy, and constitutionally-established church. Our puritan fathers did˙their full share of this sort of legal compulsion for moral ends. The right to drink or not drink liquors is an individual right, just as much as eating is individual, though the whole population should hover between dyspepsy and apoplexy.

However unwise the abstinents might be as citizens, they were at least consistent with their own moral purpose and intention toward the state. If every one had thought just as they thought, a statute of prohibition might have been maintained. If a very large majority had sincerely held the abstinent view, and had effectively abstained from any use of liquors, the law could have been administered as well as other laws on which the whole community agree. The law against killing, for example, is not perfect; but it is maintained, and even the classes restrained would hardly think of repealing it.

There was no majority either for abstinence

or for abusing drink. There were small minorities at either end of the moral and social
scale ; these classes knew their own mind.
The abstinents said, in the old Mosaic spirit,
" Thou shalt not drink," [1] and enforced the pre-
cept by their own example. The intemperates
said, " Drink, we will." Either of these classes,
generally speaking, cared more for their own will
in this question than for any other issue of
politics. It was a political motive to them,
because the consciousness of each individual
was so much excited in opposite directions : one
toward drink, the other toward abstinence.
The question never came to a square issue as
other political topics have done in our history.
Between the two minorities was an overwhelming majority of temperates. This majority made
the main bulk of the political parties, — Whig,
Anti-slavery, Democrat, or Republican. The

---

[1] There is no essential reason why the word "drink" or
"drinking habits" should be referred to alcoholic liquors
rather than to other liquids. This use is so well established,
and will save so much circumlocution, that the writer will
accept it, though it is vulgar.

compact body of abstinence voters brought a terrible pressure to bear on this great mass of citizens always moving at half-tide on the moral question of temperance or abstinence. These temperates had political motives strong in themselves and in their kind. The Whig desired his measures, the Democrat wanted his, the Republican would prohibit slavery, the Conservative would save the Union, and all were working through that common machinery of parties and political agitation which must always work out politico-moral issues. Between these various and fiery political passions, the earnest abstinents played about, log-rolling hither and thither. When there was no state-movement there would be small " pipe-laying " in the towns; combinations with a fraction of either party for or against an individual candidate; voting tickets split in such a manner as to refract a shade of one partisan against a bit of the shadow of another aspirant, until the political vision of a plain man was shaken into all the colors of the kaleidoscope.

It is not too much to say that for a generation every decent politician, clear-headed enough to see the results of politics, has lived in mortal fear of " temperance " and liquor-dealing policy. Any disinterested party leader will say, as numbers have told the writer, that politics were corrupted and dragged into the mire by these contending agitators. It is well for moralists to remember, that while we cry out for statesmen, and censure mere politicians, it is by politicians only that state movements are worked out. Statesmen are rare in any country and any time, and they reach the citizen and voter only by the help of politicians. If Abraham Lincoln had not been an adroit politician, as well as a far-seeing statesman, he never would have led the American people through a struggle as great in its moral issues as it was in its political results.

Abstinents could not see this principle, — would not see it: they were intent on a great moral purpose. What mattered a little more or little less corruption, where all was corrupt?

Your transcendental moralist, breathing the eternal ether of goodness, sees no practical difference between gold alloyed with silver and gold alloyed with lead ; they are all one in the market where all metals are as dross. The fierce abstinent said to the temperate, Whatever you claim for your own individual right, do you believe the state has a right to make drunkards, to make paupers and criminals, to license iniquity? It was decent to answer, No. Politically stupid as it was, legally illogical and dogmatic as it was, it became respectable for the average voter to answer, No. "Then vote prohibition," the men who were in earnest said, and as earnestness always carries force, they had their way. The men who should have known better had their minds filled by other and natural political interests, so they never actually grappled with this legislative liquor agitation as its importance demanded. Besides, there were many motives combining to bewilder the temperance voter. If he did not like the political issue offered by the abstinent, he liked still less to be classed with the liquor-dealing, liquor-guzzling interest. If not quite harmonizing with the one, he could not, consistently with his own average action, go with the other. Then, as mentioned above, there was a sort of bewildered *laissez-faire* morality in putting the dreadful question away from the individual. To consolidate the lazy, half-hearted emotion which was excited by the appeals of abstinents and abstaining inebriates into some sort of law, which the state should be responsible for, and which society might possibly work out, was to get rid of an ugly question within.

Thus statute after statute was invented or evolved; broken, tinkered, and refitted; damaged, whetted, and repaired, through a sickening cycle of political history.

No one changed his habits by reason of his vote for a liquor law. There was no moral responsibility for the rank and file in voting at the polls. A voted for Jones because he was "sound on the goose," and Jones was committed to a small caucus of abstinence managers.

B voted for Jones because it was respectable, and our church generally supported him. Thus Jones, and more Joneses, big and little, went up to the legislature, politically drugged; senseless under an anæsthetic worse than opium or brandy. To corrupt a citizen is bad enough; to corrupt a legislature is to spoil the chief source of citizens, — the laws under which they develop.

There was no strict moral accountability in it all. Neither A nor B changed his habits because he had voted for Jones, nor did Jones change his. Each ordered his case of wine or bought his bottle of whiskey just as coolly as if he had not stood for the principle of absolute prohibition at the polls. ' If the laws meant any thing, if there was any thing under the prohibition talk, the meaning was that the traffic should be stopped. Perhaps the voter went to his apothecary's and certified to a constructive lie, that he wanted a bottle of liquor " for medicinal or mechanical use," and piously thanked heaven he was not like the vagabond seller or

2

drinker, who broke the law at the corner. Yet A and B knew, Jones knew; Jones knew that A and B knew when they voted that, they never meant to execute the statute as they enforced the laws against stealing. Suppose Jones had been caught breaking a bank vault, after legislating on robbery, would any sane voter think of sending him to make laws again?

It is this befogging of the political intellect, this stupefaction of the moral consciousness by drugging it with political impossibility; it is these things that the writer would ask candid and thoughtful persons to consider. We hold that the abstinents, inspired by a noble and passionate emotion, capable of enormous moral influence, have prostituted it in chasing an *ignis fatuus* through the mire of politics. We hold that the temperates, halting in their opinions, inconstant in moral purpose, bewildered in political sense, have vainly tried to impose a despotism upon citizens equal before the law. We lay down the following propositions: —

I. Temperance and abstinence in regard to liquors are not similar nor convertible terms. They represent two distinct principles of living, however they may be named. These two principles should be equal before the law of the state.

II. The true province of legislation lies in the abuse of liquors, or in the abuse of the drinker. The use of liquors belongs to the individual, and lies beyond legislation.

III. Prohibition is based on the theory that all use of liquors, except for medicinal, mechanical, chemical, or artistic purposes, is wrong. This theory cannot be established either by science[1] or in the facts of the living of the people. A law so badly conceived cannot be executed.

IV. Prohibition refuses to recognize the natural laws, stated above in I., and it has failed. The statutes are not executed in any fair sense, or as other penal laws are executed.

[1] See Appendix. We have not exhausted a topic which would require a volume ; but the reader will find ample proofs of this position, drawn from unquestioned scientific authorities.

V. Laws ill grounded and ill executed cause the worst immorality in the state.

The writer would gladly have treated the subject in the order of the foregoing analysis. To his mind, the reasons which obtain against prohibition are inherent, growing out of the nature of the system itself. But long experience has established the truth, that the most effective mode of discussion is to state the facts, then the theories and expositions which those facts suggest.

We shall, therefore, state the principles of temperance and abstinence which issue in the theories of license and prohibition; and give some of the most essential facts of prohibitory legislation as they have occurred.

We will then review the claims of prohibition from the stand-point of those who made and sustain the laws ; and afterward consider the principles of prohibition and regulation from our own point of view.

We shall then detail a better system, or one which, in our opinion, has a fair chance of success.

Lastly, we shall examine the whole matter of this legislation in the light of the harm it has done, or from the ground of that morality which is the basis of all law.

TEMPERANCE AND ABSTINENCE.

THE writer has been publicly censured for his use of the word " temperance " as distinguished from " abstinence." The dispute shows that the ideas embodied in the words are ill-defined and not clearly established in the minds of many who use them. We believe that the moral state, or, as our French friends would say, the *morale* of society, will be bettered when all interested settle and define their own meaning and their own practice regarding the use of liquors. If society means temperance, let it say so ; if it means abstinence, let it say so ; nothing is to be gained by substituting the one idea or word for the other.

Shakspeare always uses the word in the meaning of the modern term, " self-control," applying it sometimes to all the passions and again to the appetites.

" What pleasure was he given to? "

"Rather rejoicing to see another merry than merry at any thing which professed to make him rejoice; a gentleman of all *temperance.*" [1]

Neither does the solid English of King James's version of the Bible ever show any confusion of these terms.

" And as he reasoned of righteousness, *temperance,* and judgment to come, Felix trembled." [2]

" But the fruit of the spirit is love, joy, peace, long-suffering, gentleness, goodness, faith, meekness, *temperance;* against such there is no law." [3]

And from the opposite direction, St. Peter indicates his notion of temperance.

" For the time past of our life may suffice us to have wrought the will of the Gentiles, when we walked in lasciviousness, lusts, excess of wine." [4] . . .

The following citations indicate the drift of the word, which, from the control of all the passions, was rather limited to the three master-

---

[1] Measure for Measure, iii. 3.   [2] Acts, xxiv. 25.
[3] Gal. v. 23.   [4] 1 Peter, iv. 3.

ing appetites of the flesh, and gradually was applied to the desires of eating and drinking almost entirely: —

" But when strong passion or weake fleshlinesse
  Would from the right way seeke to draw him wide,
  He would through *temperance* and stedfastnesse,
  Teach him the weak to strengthen, and the strong
    suppress."

  SPENSER, *Færie Queene*, II. c. 4.

"This blessed company of virtues, in this wise assembled, followeth *temperance*, as a sad and discreet matron and reverent governess, awaiting diligently, that in any wise voluptie or concupiscence have no pre-eminence in the soul of man." — SIR T. ELYOT, *The Governor*.

"For virtue (quoth Ariston the Chian), which concerneth and considereth what we ought either to do or not to do, beareth the name of prudence; when it ruleth and ordereth our lust or concupiscence, limiting out a certain measure and lawful proportion of time unto pleasures, it is called *temperance*." — HOLLAND'S *Plutarch*.

" Drink not the third glass, which thou canst not tame,
  When once it is within thee ; but before
  Mayst rule it as thou list."

  GEO. HERBERT : *The Church Porch*.

" *Temperance* permits us to take meat and drink not only as physic for hunger and thirst, but also

2*   C

as an innocent cordial and fortifier against the evils
of life, or even sometimes, reason not refusing that
liberty, merely as a matter of pleasure." — WOLLAS-
TON, *Religion of Nature.*

> " But knowledge is as food, and needs no less
>   Her *temperance* over appetite, to know
>   In measure what the mind may well contain."
>
> *Paradise Lost.*

Addison is discoursing upon eating and drinking when he says : —

"It is impossible to lay down any determinate
rule for *temperance,* because what is luxury in one
may be temperance in another."[1]

Hardly any of us would accept Addison for
a guide in this direction ; but his literary sense
is always sure and safe.

Old Elyot defines abstinence so severely, that
it would deprive our total abstinence friends of
the virtue of their abnegation while a prohibitory law is in force.

"*Abstinence* is whereby a man refraineth from
any thing which he may lawfully take."

Cowper, in more modern thought, expresses

---

[1] Spectator, 195.

the plain sense of the word as it prevails in our daily use : —

> " Call'd to the temple of impure delight,
> He that *abstains*, and he alone, does right."

This is the common sense of Christianity at this moment. If a thing is bad in itself, let it alone; if a thing is necessary in reasonable living, then it is not bad. The contrast between the two words is sharply drawn by Gibbon in his portrait of the philosopher and ascetic emperor, Julian : —

> "The *temperance* which adorned the severe manners of the soldier and philosopher was connected with some strict and frivolous rules of religious *abstinence*, and it was in honor of Pan . . . that Julian, on particular days, denied himself the use of some particular food."

If there is any other use of the words in standard writers previous to this century, or before the abstinence reform began, the writer in diligent search has been unable to find it. The two principles are different, and the reformers were wise when they abandoned the great word " temperance," which is general, and laid their demands on the limited virtue of " abstinence," which is more easily defined and capable of stricter enforcement. But having changed the basis of the regimen, it is impossible to claim both words for the one system. Else why was " abstinence " substituted, and riveted down by the binding adjective total?

Abstinence is a sound virtue, but restricted; it is in itself a passion, a strong, narrow motive, limited, from the nature of the case. To put it into the place of temperance, which controls all the passions as well as appetites, is like putting a shrivelled and ascetic monk into the form of the wide-natured Bayard or Sidney. These exclusive and dogmatic traits beget a certain arrogance in the abstinent party, which it behooves all true men to repel, and to force back into the region of impertinence, where it belongs.

When the writer read his paper at Saratoga, directed against prohibitory laws, but not against temperance or abstinence, on coming back to the floor of the convention, a person in the next seat said to him, " You mean to kick up a row, I suppose. You've no principle about it." The man was a stranger, and judging from appearance, decent enough in the ordinary relations of life. There was nothing in the character of the essay, and the writer's wife assures. him there is nothing in his personal make-up, which should lead a stranger to suppose that he was an unprincipled man in any relation, however mistaken he might be. If he had offered a bank-note at the United States Hotel, and had argued it was good, even though it should finally have been proven to be bad, strangers would hardly have thought it necessary to assume that he was uttering counterfeit money without principle. This worthy stranger had schooled himself into the notion that one virtue was all virtue, and that any person differing must, in consequence, be a bad man, whatever his life might be. That is exactly what abstinence is not, by any rule of philosophy ever invented. It is the result of a powerful feeling, the reaction from one dangerous appetite; it is not an Aaron's rod which shall swallow up every other power in human nature.

We are not striving to make points against abstinence. The writer thoroughly believes that good morals will be advanced when worthy men clarify their ideas and bring their principles to the bar of common reason. We, who hold to the doctrine of temperance, are entitled to decent respect from the abstinents in the discussion, and we will have it. The burden of proof is not yet removed from the abstinents; they have never yet reformed a society and brought it into such practical accord with their system that they can claim that system to be the only rule of life, and then abuse every person who differs from their opinion.

Much has been accomplished by the total abstinence reform in New England; whether some similar results could not have been brought about by simpler means is matter of

doubt. We do not mean to argue by implica-
tion against the system ; we only suggest that
it is not the only method of temperance, and
should at least be modest until it shows a
society reasonably reformed, and not held in
the grip of a tyrannical law, under which it
writhes and shrinks. Plenty of facts illustrate
this individual and exceptional character of the
abstinence system. It has no social force except through tyranny, as we shall prove farther
on. If abstinence were the best living, then its
votaries should live by themselves. Accordingly they tried " temperance hotels." They
all failed. If abstinence were the safest living,
then a life insurance association on that basis
ought to be the best. The Phœnix Company
of Hartford attempted to found its business on
totally abstinent lives. It was ably managed,
but languished. The same managers changed
the basis to " temperate " lives, and achieved a
great success. We can learn of no other experiment where any company confined itself to
insuring abstinents.

No greater reform than the change made in the drinking habits of the upper classes of England, has ever been perfected. It is not necessary to go back to Fielding, with his Squire Westerns and drinking chaplains. Take the testimony of one whose life reached over into our own time. Lord Brougham is writing of the scenes at the funeral of his maternal grandfather. These persons were the better sort of people in northern England and southern Scotland. Brougham's mother was the sister of the historian Robertson : —

"The Duke of Norfolk began the toasts at the funeral. Many toasts followed. The guests drank long and deeply. The funeral then proceeded on its way to the parish church . . . the road winding along the steep banks of the river Eamont. Arrived at the church, the hearse was met by the rector, but the coffin had disappeared. The shock was enough to sober the merry mourners. On searching back, the coffin was discovered in the river, into which it had fallen, pitched down the steep bank. . . . The shock and the scandal produced by all this had the effect not only of sobering everybody, but of putting an end to such disgraceful orgies in the county for the future."— *Life and Times of Lord Brougham, by himself.* I. 19.

An Irish wake and funeral had a similar accident in the suburbs of Providence not long since, except that they were lucky enough to land the dead subject on a hard turnpike road, and not at the bottom of a river.

Take Brougham's own experience when yachting among the Western Islands about the beginning of this century: —

"Every morning we shoot grouse, hares, snipes, and deer, till five o'clock, then eat the most luxurious dinners of game and fish, drinking claret, champagne, hermitage, and hock; at night we are uniformly and universally *dead* (drunk). Your humble servant being in the chair (*ex officio*), does his best, and, having a good capacity enough for wine, does odd enough things. Yesterday our mess fell off; Campbell and I and two natives set into it, and among four had twelve port bottles; the natives and Bob being stowed away, I finished another bottle and a half of port with an old exciseman, major of the volunteers. This morning I found all Stornaway in full tongue at my astonishing feat; went to the moors, walked

it off, and killed a brace of hares at one dis-
charge.

(Signed)   HENRY BROUGHAM."
Life and Times, I., 85.

In England, to-day, the nobles, gentry, commercial, professional, and upper classes generally, with the better sort of workingmen,
are as temperate as any equal number of
people in any country; we should ourselves
think they are more temperate. They use
liquors socially; but the abuse is rare. It is
not decent now for a gentleman to be drunk,
— and by gentleman we mean a dignified
man; a little man or a workingman may be a
man of dignity; but one hundred years since,
as Brougham's letter to his friends at home,
as well as all literature, shows, it was a very
respectable thing for a young man to exhibit
the powers of his body in a struggle with the
bottle, or such a number of bottles as he was
equal to. Prohibitory laws have not changed
these people; nor has the feeling of total abstinence worked the change in the habits and

tone of the aristocracy. The whole bearing of society has changed; and temperance in every appetite has become the practice as well as the aspiration of those persons whose social position makes them a law unto themselves. Compare the sovereigns of the Teutonic races two centuries ago with those of this time. In this case kings are types of their times. New vices have been developed in modern times; but the strength of many old ones has been subdued. Material wealth and comfort have increased so rapidly, and diffused themselves so much, that excess of appetite is not now the main desire of man, as it often was in a coarser time. To control the appetites in every direction, to practise a balanced temperance, is the aspiration of large classes of society; and in England it has become the practice of those we have mentioned.

Arthur Arnold, in the "Fortnightly," shows that England is much more temperate than she was a century since: —

" We do not, in the reign of Queen Victoria, consume one-half as much beer as we did in that of Queen Anne. The average consumption of malt per head of the population was — it will be seen from the following table, taken from authentic records — considerably more than twice as great in the middle of the eighteenth century as in that of the nineteenth. From 1740 to 1790 it was : —

1740	. .	3.78	1760	. .	4.29	1780	. .	3.94
1750	. .	4.85	1770	. .	3.38	1790	. .	2.57

"From 1801 to 1871 it was : —

1801	. . .	1.20	1841	. . .	1.35
1811	. . .	1.60	1851	. . .	1.50
1821	. . .	1.38	1861	. . .	1.61
1831	. . .	1.63	1871	. . .	1.72

"John Barleycorn is therefore far less powerful in the nineteenth than in the preceding century, — and why? He was partially upset by John Chinaman. I think the fact is indisputable. In the time of the Tudors beer was drunk at every meal; there was a steady drinking from breakfast to supper. As compared with that time, the draught of malt liquor has declined more than one-half, otherwise there could not have been the enormous consumption of tea. The British people now consume very nearly four pounds of tea per head per annum, — an amount which has steadily progressed while the consumption per head of malt has been all but stationary. This fact is interesting, if only because it shows that it is possible, by the introduction of new drinks and by legislation, to change the bibulous habits of a people."

We beg our abstinence friends to consider the signs of the times. Look at the course of New England in regard to social amusements. It is not toward severity and asceticism, but toward liberty and well-regulated use of social pleasures. This does not indicate a popular mood which will bear too much pressure from the ascetic side. Least of all, if we are in earnest in trying to restrain drunkenness, should the abstinent party repel and censure that portion of society which, while using liquors, would have strong influence in controlling their abuse, if that influence could be fairly exerted.

Many good people choose their course in this matter not according to their own wish or conviction, but according to the supposed effect that course may produce on others. Persons who are not convinced of the wrong in drink-

ing, yet avoid it because of the effect their
example may have on other and weaker ones.
In so far as this is a genuine affection for abstinence, it carries some weight and has some
social influence; but when it is a mere fashion
of morals, adopted not for its own excellence
but for its external effect, it is either useless
or injurious, as we hope to show.

There are two kinds of example one negative, as when we say with Othello, in his passionate condemnation of Cassio, " I'll make
thee an example;" or the positive sort, when we
"propound to ourselves some exemplar saint."
The abstinent exemplars do not adopt either
kind. We form ourselves on a good man because we admire his virtues, and strive to
model the same traits in our own character.
Of course this process, if successful, carries us
into the essence of the saint, into the secret
of his being. No one ever created virtue
from the outside, or by imitating its effects;
if he prevails over it, he seizes it in the germ;
and having become fired by the same causes

which inspired the saint, he puts forth equal effects. This theory of perfunctory example attempts to bring people to abstinence, not through a serious conviction in those who practise it, but through the form and external custom which that practice has put on. It fails, and it deserves failure. The parsimonious, wealthy parent, who limits his own expenditure to make a model for his son's imitation, generally comes out with a spendthrift heir. In his heart the boy despises the father because he is playing a part before him. If the boy is not capable in his more ardent and generous nature of the same passion for money which the parent feels, he cannot cultivate it by imitation. The real object of the father is avarice; the object he represents to the boy is prudence and economy. The boy, generally speaking, is not capable of avarice, and the artificial pressure intended to create prudence recoils into extravagance. The theory fails and, we say, deserves to fail, for it begins by confounding definite and important principles.

Ethical truths cannot be divided and twisted, and spun into new threads of truth by any expert exercise of diplomatic art. Men may get property, or get on in life, according to Mr. Disraeli, and states may be governed, by other forces be-sides moral ones. This involves other questions not properly belonging here. But in moral influences we have a new and simple creation in every act. The individual takes close hold of his neighbor, and there is hand-to-hand work. The highest and lowest intelligences are equal here. Take up the most ignorant rustic, and he knows whether you mean just what the words you tell him would indicate. If deceived by circumstance the first time, he will detect you in the second instance. Every man is his own mirror, and this revealing of the individual is all that can be done in example. If you reveal something else, and send forth an image which does not proceed from your central and deepest conviction, then you create a bad example, though your intention may be good apparently. You can sustain but one ideal at a time, and are fortunate if you have moral energy enough for that. It must be the best you have; and the best you can do for another is the very best you can do for yourself. No constructive ideal, made from several nicely-balanced motives, will affect your neighbor, or, if it affects him at all, the effect will be bad. Bear in mind this is not hypocrisy, it is not a deception of others, but the much more subtle deceiving of ourselves. The cynic Rochefoucauld said: " It is as easy to deceive one's self without perceiving it, as it is difficult to deceive others without their perceiving it."

If a man looks over his consciousness, and finds that he has no fixed principles of abstinence, then, looking to the interests of society, he had better practise temperance, and leave abstinence to those persons who believe in it, and would die for it, if necessary. That is the best example which exhibits whatever he would sustain with all his might. In actual fact, a man says feebly: " This is not wrong, but I may be misunderstood, and it is better for me to deny

myself than to make others offend." The mis-
understanding begins with himself, and grows
larger the farther it extends. The motive behind the self-denial is not the motive which
impelled St. Paul, but is the nerveless lack of
courage which will not let a man work out his
own convictions. It is this sort of example
which grinds the individuality out of us. It
examples the aquiline nose into a Grecian, the
Roman into a pug, and soon would leave not a
nose on our socially smooth faces.

In another view of this subject, example de-
feats itself. Truth-speaking is a good example,
but any thing spoken for an example is not the
truth. Truth is imperial, and compels the individual to follow her behest with no reference
to consequence or the needs of any other individual. In the same manner, good morals are
impelled by the good sense and wisdom of the
individual working his whole nature from its
own centre: else the sense becomes folly, and
the morals become false and vicious in their
effects. If we are told, this is hard for the weak

ones who follow examples mechanically, and, by exceeding the example of temperance, fall into drunkenness, we answer, that we cannot help it. You cannot aid a fool by taking up folly, or by denying an appetite in order to keep him from abusing that appetite. If the appetite is unlawful in itself, that is another question, which this argument does not include. South says: " One thing receives another, not according to the full latitude of the object, but according to the scanty model of its own capacity." Excessive drinking, from one point of view, is an insanity of the' appetite. To treat the appetites of all individuals as if they were insane, brings on the same confusion that we should have if we adapted our common living to the needs of persons mentally insane. We should then make ourselves crazy, without helping the few insane who require a special treatment.

All this confusion arises from the effort to put the test of our moral conduct in the wrong place.

" As a true balance is neither set right by a true

one, nor judged by a false one; so likewise a just person has neither to be set right by just persons, nor to be judged by unjust ones." — *Epictetus* (Higginson's Trans., p. 414).

Our example is not the main test and standard of our lives: it is a mere index, which shows what our living is. It must be true, so far as it goes; but the proper interpretation of the index is not a social matter for the public; it is an individual matter for ourselves. The test — the great plummet and plumb-line of our living — is in our interior relation with God; not conscience alone, but all the faculties of which conscience is the expositor. When this great test is straight and satisfied, then example will take care of itself, and other persons will receive no harm from it. For even if the example be one which others ought not to follow, it will be thoroughly sincere, and something which carries conviction or repulsion with it. Then one with the meanest comprehension can follow, or take warning and avoid; for he will understand, as we instanced in the case of our rustic, who knows our truth or falsehood at once.

Physical illustrations never wholly fit, but there is a close analogy to the sailing of a ship in this conduct of the individual. In steering a ship, there are three main elements, — the rudder, the compass, and the course chosen or indicated. The winds and resisting currents enter also, but in this connection we treat them as a part of the rudder or steering process. The captain compares information, adjusts observations, and cultivates good fellowship with other vessels; but he never changes his own course a point on account of others. If they need aid, he assists, but never links his own craft to one water-logged, nor carries more or less sail for the benefit of another. The moment he should divert his course for the bearing it may have on another, he would become a silly man as well as a poor navigator. To do otherwise would be putting his own compass, or course of sailing, as it might be, on board another vessel. The individual sails by his conscience, which is the best index of right and wrong, and quickest brings the ship to her due bearings. But his course is adjusted through other faculties, as we said before, forming a great ocean in the soul of mankind, through which from day to day the individual works his way. Justice, reverence, truth, fortitude, patience, temperance, and a hundred other moral virtues, enter into the course of living, and influence it now this way and now that. The man gathers information wherever he can, takes his observations warily and sincerely, but he must take them for himself, and adjust his own course by the compass of his conscience and the great test of righteous living, which brings him near, and keeps him in harmony with God, the Father of his soul: When he puts this test, this plummet of his own righteousness, into somebody else's ship, into an external form of example, then he has lost his own positive course in life without aiding or changing the course of others.

It was necessary to make this apparent digression, for the principle lies near the core of our main topic. Temperance or abstinence in respect to liquors are principles strictly within the domain of each individual. Each man has a right — morally, so long as no law of God is broken, which we show in another chapter; socially, as we have proved in the foregoing — to choose for himself whether he will use or refuse liquors. The abuse of liquors at once carries the individual beyond himself, and creates the right of social interference. Consequently, the use or non-use of liquors should be equal before the law; and there is no just reason for interfering by legislation or legal process with either practice.

THE WORKING OF PROHIBITION.

THE abstinence reformers sincerely believed that the law only lacked power; if they could have greater force at their command, then they thought they could abolish the traffic in liquors. This feeling was general among them, and it was not a new discovery, but a practical application of this supposed principle, which Neal Dow accomplished in the famous Maine Law. This was introduced shortly into other States, and became the political shibboleth of the abstinence party. It proceeded against the property as well as the offender under the law, and gave stringent power of seizure. This statute was enacted in Rhode Island in 1852, and it is interesting to review some of the arguments which were used in obtaining it, because they are the same in kind which prevail with the whole party.

Amos C. Barstow led the reformers, and we cite from his speech in the Rhode Island House of Representatives, as reported in the " Providence Journal " : —

"We are acting on a petition of 25,000 persons, of whom 11,500 are adult male citizens; they embrace a large part of the moral worth of the State. . . . These petitions bear the names of the learned and excellent President of your University, of ministers of religion, of your physicians, merchants. . . . They represent the *industry* and the *virtue* of the State. I beg gentlemen who are preparing amendments to this bill to mark the prayer of these petitions. They want a law to SUPPRESS the rum traffic, — not to *regulate*, but to SUPPRESS. They ask for nothing more, and will be content with nothing less. . . . I charge the *evils* of intemperance upon this traffic, — and for this reason, the appetite is not *natural* but *acquired*, and acquired through the temptations presented by this traffic. The only way, therefore, to stop the demand is to cut off the supply.

" Our present laws do not, and cannot, suppress it, and for these reasons : —

" 1st. It requires more evidence to convict a man under them·than would be sufficient to hang him.

" 2d. The penalties are inadequate. So true is this,

3*

that, in my opinion, the law is hardly worth enforcing. It only serves, when enforced, to fret and goad the rumseller, while it allows the traffic to go on. He can pay its penalties, and grow rich in spite of it.

"3d. It allows towns to license the traffic. The State thus, by giving this liberty, sanctions the traffic, and becomes a party to the crime. . . .

"It is hoped that these (*i.e.*, provisions of new statute) and other stringent provisions will secure the desired end, — will suppress this traffic. The success which has thus far attended the enaction of the law in Maine warrants this hope."

After twenty-two years' experience of this statute, during which time it has either slept on the statute-book or been enforced in feverish spells of energy, we are still hearing the same arguments and the same promises, with the demand for more power in the law. The only new principle introduced into the prohibitory statutes of Rhode Island or Massachusetts has been in the appointment of a force of state constables. These officers, it was claimed, having no local associations, would enforce the law more strictly.

The reader will observe the principles which run through this argument. The state must take control of the appetites of its citizens just as a mother directs an infant. Then, these appetites are not in the individual, but "*acquired*" through the agency of the liquor-seller, and the state must suppress the traffic in order to cut off the appetite. Many promises made by the abstinence advocates were even stronger than those we have cited, which were tempered by the opposition of debate. There was a serious conviction among the majority that a new era in the temperance reformation had arrived, and that well-disposed persons, whatever their private desires, should lend a hand to bring in the promised millennium. The "industry and virtue" of the Maine Law people was tacitly backed by the larger force of "world's people," who, though not allowed the sanctimonious crown of virtue, yet try to do their duty toward their neighbors and the state. Every assistance was rendered to the abstinence managers after the law was enacted, and many doubtful ones even voted for it, that the principle might be tried. Mr. Barstow, the ablest executive in the abstinence party, was elected mayor of the city of Providence, and a complete staff of officers was made out, who should in principle sympathize with the statute. The " world's people " laid in demijohns of spirits and cases of wine, until every other house was not only a castle, but a castle supplied against a siege.

The results did not justify the ample preparation made for the law. Illicit traffic among the lower classes began at once, and defied the best exertions of the officers. Clubs were formed among well-to-do persons, and the drinking of liquors kept on. All who have observed these clubbing operations to avoid a law — abstinence men as well as temperates — agree that they are among the worst evils society ever brought in upon itself. We give the testimony of a thoroughly disinterested gentleman who is used to the observation of facts, and knows how to reduce them to a scientific verity.

"Providence, Oct. 21, 1874.

" Wm. B. Weeden, Esq.:

"My Dear Sir,—In accordance with your request, I send you in writing the substance of the statement made by me orally to you a few days ago.

"During the years 1854–5–6, I was living in one of the principal cities of Connecticut, and was very favorably situated to observe the workings of the 'Maine Law,' when first passed and enforced in that State. The evils resulting from it were so serious, that those of its most ardent supporters who were really in a position to see and feel the real state of the case were quite willing to allow the law — *in that city at least* — to become a dead letter.

"On one occasion, I heard the prosecuting attorney (who had been very earnest in working to secure the passage of the law) state the following facts in private conversation : —

"'No sooner were the dram-shops closed than the regular tipplers, uniting, formed various "clubs" or "societies" ostensibly for social or literary purposes. Rooms were hired, fitted up in good style, and stocked with an abundance of the "ardent," purchased at wholesale prices in New York. The rooms, open at all times to members, became their favorite resort at night, and gambling soon became a marked feature of their festive gatherings. Not satisfied with fleecing one another, they soon began to draw in fresh victims,—the more innocent the better. Young men, who would have turned with disgust from a dram-shop, were easily enticed into a "club-room," and those who would never have consented to play at cards in a public resort were more ready to join in a game, "among friends, you know." The infection quietly spread, especially among employés of the higher class, — clerks and others holding positions of trust, who had been considered above all suspicion. At length the employers became aware that things were going wrong, and soon discovered the source of the evil. Urgent appeals were made to the prosecuting attorney by many of the best citizens — most of whom had been zealous and influential friends of the Maine Law — to put an end to the pressure which gave these "clubs" their being and their vitality. The law soon ceased to be enforced, but its evil effects long survived, as the "clubs," once organized, maintained themselves for some time. Many a young man, armed at all points against open temptations, succumbed to the insidious lure of a "secret society," with its promise of a social circle of "good fellows." That these "clubs" were really the result of the law, and that they owed their vitality in great measure to its enforcement, is, I think, capable of distinct proof.'"

The experience of clubs of this sort has been equally bad everywhere, though they have not all tended so much toward gambling. A disinterested witness, who had an intimate knowledge of the habits of the working people in Connecticut at this time, assured the writer that many persons and families bought supplies of whiskey from carts which came in the night, who hardly drank at all in ordinary seasons. The feeling was rife among them that they were cut off from a right, and must make it up from the first illicit opportunity afforded.

The writer was then a clerk, and often at work in different warehouses with the wharf laborers. When the enforcement of the law was most rigid, and a stranger might suppose there was not even a dew-drop of whiskey accessible, these men would leave their work, one at a time, dive into some cavern or burrow, and return in five minutes, their lips wet with the hasty dram. These men had as little power to evade the law as any class could have. It is fair to infer that others of the same kind and other classes attained the same privileges elsewhere. All external evidence showed that Mr.

Barstow's argument should be reversed. Instead of the supply of liquor being the cause of an appetite, facts indicated that the appetite commanded its supply in spite of all the power the city of Providence could bring to suppress it.

"As they (statesmen) descend from the state to a province, from a province to a parish, and from a parish to a private house, they go on accelerated in their fall. They ought to know the different departments of things, — what belongs to laws, and what manners alone can regulate. To these, great politicians may give a leaning, but they cannot give a law." — BURKE, V. 210 (Rivingtons).

The results among the better conditioned people were patent to every one. The abstinence administration was turned out as a failure, and matters drifted along in the old way. It might be expected that the dangerous classes — those who are directly amenable to the law, through lack of character and settled place in life — might be controlled more surely than the wealthy, or those humble laborers whom we have instanced above. That the system failed here also, the testimony of Dr. Wayland shows.

He became an abstinence man, on account of the weight his character and public position gave to his example. He afterward lent his influence to prohibition, in the hope that it might prevail; he was a petitioner for the law, as we have seen, though he always doubted its final success. The writer is assured of this by those who knew him well.

˜ The report of the State Prison Inspectors, drawn in the handwriting of Dr. Wayland, — he being chairman, — dated Jan. 14, 1853, contains the following : —

"It will be seen, from the above statistics, that the greater part of the expense to which the State is at present subjected in maintaining the prison, arises from the county jail. If this branch of the prison could be made sufficiently productive, the condition of the establishment would be much more satisfactory. The reasons why the earnings of the county jail are so small are twofold. In the first place, those persons who are only detained for trial are not subjected to labor, and hence there are no means for reducing the expenses of their maintenance; and, secondly, the sentences to the county jail are, in many cases, so short, that no time is allowed for teaching these convicts any profitable labor.

"The bad effect of these short sentences is not confined to its expense of maintenance. It is thus rendered impossible to teach the convicts habits of industry, or to overcome habits of intemperance; and, still more, by returning the same convicts frequently to prison, there is entailed upon the State a large expense in the shape of fees of arrest, commitment, and trial." (The state had just added a wing to the state prison, containing eighty-eight cells. The average number of prisoners was then one hundred and fifteen, — forty-seven being state and sixty-eight jail prisoners.)

"The Inspectors respectfully request that any part of the State Prison may be used as a county jail at the pleasure of the Board." — *Acts and Resolves.* Rhode Island, Jan., 1853, p. 332.

On the 31st of December, 1855, about three and a half years after the Maine Law went into operation, the State Prison Inspectors made another report, which also bears the name of Dr. Wayland. We extract: —

"By this mode of exercising criminal jurisprudence, no single object is attained; nothing is done either to diminish the amount of crime or to im-

prove the individual criminal. The result may
therefore be set down as nothing. . . . This total
$6,306.49 is the cost in Providence county for in-
toxication, which is taken from the pockets of the
tax-payers. From these statistics it would seem,
then, that the amount paid by the county of Providence alone for imprisonment for intoxication, if
divided among the several towns of the State,
would furnish each one with about $200 for the
purchase of a library. As at present expended, it
is impossible to discover that it attains a single val-
uable result. . . . The last report for the Albany
Penitentiary has been received. The experience of
that institution has been in every respect so nearly
identical with our own, that we beg the attention
of the Assembly to the following extract : —

   " ' ALBANY PENITENTIARY REPORT. — Since the enactment of what is termed the " Prohibitory Law," a
new crime, denominated " public intoxication," punishable by ten days' imprisonment, has been instituted, the
practical effect of which has been detrimental to the
pecuniary interests of the penitentiary. With the law
itself the Inspectors have nothing to do, whatever their
individual opinion of its merits or demerits may be. . . .
If our law-makers had intended to punish the tax-payer
instead of the drunkard, or, rather, if they had meant to
inflict a slight punishment on the latter at the expense
of the former class, the object could not have been more
effectually accomplished. Neither is its moral influence
in any degree salutary. In the opinion of the Inspect-

ors, the statute referred to should be so amended as to lengthen the term of imprisonment, or things in this respect restored to their original state, and offenders treated as they were before the law existed.'

"Impressed with these convictions, the Board of Inspectors ask leave to commend the laws relating to imprisonment in the jail to the attention of the General Assembly, fully convinced that they will, in their wisdom, originate such enactments as will more effectually and economically accomplish the object of criminal jurisprudence."—*Acts and Resolves.* Rhode Island Assembly, Jan., 1856.

A nuisance act was passed in 1856, which supplemented the original law, and corrected some of its details which had been damaged in the courts. But the practical results, after all the legislative tinkering, were no better than the old system before the Maine Law began. Mr. Barstow's description of the old law — "it only serves, when enforced, to fret and goad the rumseller while it allows the traffic to go on; he can pay its penalties and grow rich in spite of it"—applies equally well to the new or Maine Law system. The liquor-dealers in Providence have acquired large fortunes, built solid blocks of stores, and in every way evinced a prosperous traffic. The extra pressure of the law has increased their margin of profit. It might be said this increased price was an advantage to the drinker, in that it checks consumption ; which would be true, were it not that the quality of the article sold has deteriorated so much from the same cause that the injury done the drinker is aggravated in a double ratio.

The writer is assured, by a competent eye-witness, one whose testimony would be weighty in any affair, that the result was substantially the same ,in Maine. Though the law maintained itself in administration, yet its fruits were not satisfactory. "After the first two years the extreme measures disgusted all moderate temperance men."

The writer supposed — every one supposes — that it would be easy to set forth these facts of the working of prohibition and of the habits of the people in their use of liquors in satisfactory statistics which should indicate the consumption of liquors. Wherever we travel, whether in Maine, Massachusetts, New York, or Ohio, we see about the same evidences of liquors and their consumption. Bar-rooms, saloons, and retail shops prevail almost equally. In large places, when new streets are opened, we see about the same preparation for liquor-selling, whether the location be in Massachusetts or New York. A village may show signs of an especial abstinence from liquors, but the next village will give equal evidence of a different habit, while both live under the same prohibitory law. States having different systems, whether of license or prohibition, show no marked difference in their drinking habits. Go into their homes, and you find abstinence prevailing among the ascetic temperaments, and about the same tendency toward drinking in different places among those who do not agree with the ascetics. It is evident, at a glance, that the law prevailing does not essentially change the habits of the people, though they may differ in degree. A notable proof of this fact from the negative side is afforded in Vineland, New Jersey. Here a large village has grown up under a prohibitory system almost absolute. The reason why the system has succeeded is because the people are different from any common town organized by the usual laws of settlement. The place was exceptionally conceived, exceptionally settled, and is exceptionally governed. It drew together a group of citizens tired of other places and desirous of new ways of living. The administration which may succeed there, is, in the nature of the case, unfit for the country at large. There could not be a whole country of Vinelands unless there were more worlds to select from. Whether the whole country would be better if it were all Vineland, we are not discussing; it would require at least three generations of people exceptionally selected and reared to prove the superiority of the exceptional system; meanwhile, it is an open question. Laws are made for the whole people, and not for any fragment, whether that exceptional portion be better or worse than the majority.

Determined to prove these plain facts, the writer applied to one of the best statisticians in Massachusetts, and drew out the following reply: —

"I profess to have the means of getting at *some* statistics; but a more preposterous request than that you sent to me yesterday I never knew. Dr. —— might tell you to a pint how much liquor was used in the State in any given period, but he would get at it in the same way the boy said the astronomers ascertained the distance to the sun, — guess at half and multiply it by two.

"No, my dear Sir, there is *no* way you can find out any thing of the kind in any trustworthy way. Some of the wholesale liquor dealers may have approximate statistics which would be useful for comparison of one year with another, on the principle that the blunders will balance, but not otherwise, — nothing absolute. You might reckon that *all* the liquor that comes into the State is used, as there is a prohibitory law in Maine, and no liquor is sold or used in that State.

"Don't be discouraged by my inability to answer this question. Try me again. — Sincerely yours."

The writer then thought a search might be made through the records of the common car-

riers, on the great lines at least, which should
show the amount of liquors carried into Boston,
for a term of years, and thus give us on paper
the relative consumption from season to season.
Such a statement would be interesting to all
who discuss this vexed question, whatever their
view of it. A gentleman much interested in
these issues, and so situated as to command all
these sources of information, replied as follows: "I have enquired both at the Providence offices and at the Boston and Albany,
to see if any such statistics as you desire are
accessible; but I find nothing less than a
most disproportionate amount of labor and
research would accomplish even an approxima-
tion to what you require, and this would be
open to criticism." We have been thus particular in detailing this experience, because it
shows the method by which we have labored
in this work. There is not a single statement
made in this whole essay which is not the result
of conference with persons who know whereof

they speak. The writer has no connection with political party or politicians, and no connection with the press. This freedom from the powers that be, in these regions of sumptuary law, has opened the mouths of many officers who could not speak in a report, in a political convention, or through the medium of the newspaper reporter. Many statements we make guardedly, for the purpose of keeping the personality of the witnesses secret. We have been received in the fullest and freest confidence, and whatever the reader may think of our argument, he may rely on the fact that the writer receives and gives out no testimony which he would not apply in his own affairs or his own family.

The present prohibitory law in Massachusetts was enacted in 1869. In principle it is like all these statutes, and like the original Maine Law; they only differ in details.

THE STATE APPOINTS A COMMISSIONER OR STATE AGENT.

CHAP. 415 — SEC. 17.[1] "The selectmen of every town containing less than 5,000 inhabitants may, the mayor and aldermen of every city or selectmen of every town containing more than 5,000 inhabitants shall, appoint one or more suitable persons as agents of such place to purchase and sell at some convenient places therein, spirituous or intoxicating liquors to be used in the arts, or for medicinal, chemical, and mechanical purposes, and no other. . . ."

SEC. 24. "Whoever, purchasing spirituous or intoxicating liquor of any agent, intentionally makes a false statement regarding the use to which the liquor is intended to be applied, shall pay a fine of not less than five nor more than twenty dollars."

SALES SPECIALLY AUTHORIZED.

SEC. 27. "The importer of liquor of foreign production may own, possess, keep, or sell the same in the original packages, and in quantities not less than the quantities in which the laws of the United States require such liquors to be imported."

SEC. 28. "Druggists may sell, for medicinal pur-

[1] General Laws of Massachusetts, June, 1869.

poses only, pure alcohol to other druggists, apothecaries, and physicians.

SEC. 29. "A chemist, artist, or manufacturer may keep for use, not for sale. Any person may manufacture or sell wine for sacramental purposes. Any person may manufacture or sell cider, not sold or kept with intent, at a public bar, to be drank on the premises."

SEC. 32. "Whoever directly or indirectly sells to another person spirituous or intoxicating liquor, or mixed liquor, part of which is spirituous or intoxicating, in violation of the provisions of this act, shall, for one violation, pay ten dollars and be imprisoned in the house of correction not less than twenty nor more than thirty days; for a second violation, shall pay twenty dollars and be imprisoned in the house of correction not less than thirty nor more than sixty days; and for any subsequent violation shall pay fifty dollars and be imprisoned in the house of correction not less than three nor more than six months."

SEC. 35. "In all cases under this act, delivery of intoxicating liquor in or from any building or place, other than a private dwelling-house or its dependencies, or in such dwelling or dependencies, if part of the same is a tavern, &c., shall be deemed *primâ facie* evidence of and punishable as a sale; and a delivery in or from a private dwelling-house, with payment implied, shall be deemed *primâ facie* evidence of and punishable as a sale."

Secs. 36, 37, 38, 39. "Whoever owns liquors with intent to sell; whoever receives the same to convey to another intending to sell; whoever receives for a railroad; whoever brings into the Commonwealth, or conveys from place to place within the same," all these are fined or imprisoned, and a railroad is to be fined fifty dollars for each offence.

Sec. 62. "All intoxicating liquors kept for sale, and the implements and vessels actually used in selling and keeping the same, contrary to the provisions of this act, are declared to be common nuisances."

Chap. 442 — Sec. 1. "The word 'constable,' wherever it occurs in Chap. 415, shall be held and construed to include within its meaning the constable of the Commonwealth and his deputies."

This act was amended eleven times in four years, or to 1873 inclusive. As the Chief of the Boston Police says : —

"The law for the suppression of the sale of intoxicating drinks is manifold in its provisions, including the single sale, the second sale, common sale, seizure, and common nuisance clauses, each with its respective penalty. . . . The duties imposed on the new organization (*i.e.,* the state constabulary) were of no inconsiderable magnitude; but it is reasonable to suppose that all officers on whom the duty devolved, faithfully carried out the policy of the authorities under whom they served; certainly a great many prosecutions have been made under all the provisions of the law by both local and *state officers; but yet drunkenness, the evil, has not diminished.*"[1]

According to the Police Report, in 1872, there were in Boston 2,768 places for the sale of liquors, or one shop for every 99 inhabitants. Providence, which at the same time had a very loose license system, reports one shop for 223 inhabitants. According to Arnold, London had 10,000 "public and beer houses," or one to about 300 inhabitants. These figures are all approximate, and the most accurate which are to be had. They show that the traffic which is cut off by prohibition in country towns is recompensed in Boston. With our abundant transportation, this transferred traffic is easily carried on.

---

[1] Report of Chief of Boston Police, 1872, p. 50. The italics are ours.

The State Board of Health of Massachusetts are equally positive in their conviction that the prohibitory law has not practically succeeded. We cite : —

"For years public sentiment in the Commonwealth has fluctuated between the extremes of action and reaction on this matter. Meanwhile, it seems certain that while throughout the State there is less drunkenness than formerly, it never was more rampant than now in Boston and some of the larger cities. This habit the Board believe to be infinitely deleterious ' to the prosperity, happiness, health, and lives of the citizens.' The records of our courts, and the knowledge which every one has of its effects in the private family, assure us of this fact. *The evil is enormous.* How to remedy it is the difficulty.[1]

In the small villages and country towns of Massachusetts, as well as Rhode Island. the law has proved more effective. Whether this success is not superficial and dearly purchased, is matter of doubt. When we dam a stream, it is not stopped; the current ceases as we

[1] Report of the State Board of Health, 1871, p. 11.

look upon it, but while the sources remain the stream gathers new force, and cuts new channels, made even more dangerous by the dam we have interposed.

Laws in this country are born out of the life of the people. In the world's history the state has never distributed its sovereignty so lavishly and freely as our American government has done. The people have great power, and their mood takes speedy effect in legislation, especially in the state organisms. Sovereignty is absolute, and knows no moral right or wrong after it has once uttered itself in a statute. Hence a statute must either be in such accord with our common living that it works itself out easily, or it will remain a dead letter, and be eddied by the popular current passing by it. The people will hardly resist it by means of the regular forms of legal resistance, for they made it. A prohibitory liquor statute carries injustice with it. The man seeking to purchase is not a criminal unless he is drunk; he finds a seller willing to take the risk of the law, and the seller is always supported by the public sentiment of that part of the community he knows most of. He is tacitly supported by the whole community; for the people who give weight to ordinary legal administration — what we term the respectable part of society — take, and will take, no practical action in liquor prosecutions. No man hesitates to inform or testify against theft or against maltreating brutes, or any other crime which common public sentiment abhors. A citizen does not like to dabble with liquor-selling; the buyers will hardly testify; hence the prosecutors resort to shifty tricks to establish their suits. The local officers are but the executive arm of their communities; they are men of like passions to those among whom they live. If it were an honorable and desirable pursuit to follow liquor-selling through its sinuous devices, they would seize upon the honor. As it is, they generally decline the opportunity.

For these reasons, the prohibitionists devised

4*   F

the state constabulary, by means of which the
odium of executing the law should be removed
from the provinces of home rule and laid
upon a central force emanating from the state.
The pressure brought to bear on these imperial
officials by the Joneses we have described, and
the abstinence politicians should be sufficient
to keep the law in operation. In a measure
the system has succeeded, for it has brought
the power of the state to bear more readily
on the details of government than we have ever
known in our American experience.   Carried
out, it would destroy town government, the cor-
ner-stone of our republic. A town not able to
administer its liquor laws wisely would soon
fail in other administration. A board of bridge-
builders, another of road-makers, another of
almshouse keepers, and another and another,
all under state control, might conduct their
first operations more wisely than the citizens
of a small and remote town might do the
same ; but, meanwhile, what would become
of the citizen on whom the town rests ? what

of the town on which the state rests? It
is the method of imperial Russia, it is the
method of France, which adapts itself equally
well to an ephemeral republic or to an empire.
It needs the virtues of a despotism as well
as its power to make it tolerable in administration. Mingle the powers of a despotism
with the vices of party politics, and the result
will not better the state, even though a few
liquor shops are closed in the process. It is
matter of common report in Massachusetts that
practices are instituted under this system which
should make all good citizens grieve, whether
they be temperate or abstinent in principle.

Both Rhode Island and Massachusetts have
good assay laws, which rest on the statute-book
with no practical results. The abstinence men
do not care to stop the sale of adulterated
liquors as such. The difference between the
good and the bad is to them, as Mr. Toots
would say, of "no consequence." Their aim
is to suppress the whole traffic, and the further
this impossible goal is removed, the more ardent

becomes their pursuit of it. Any practicable regulation to cut off present evils moves them to tacit opposition, or, at best, to indifference.

In Rhode Island, the old Maine Law of 1852, with its amendments, was allowed to sleep on the statute-book, the legislature meanwhile granting privileges for local license to the towns and cities. In May, 1874, the General Assembly repealed all the license laws, re-established the original seizure powers of the Neal Dow law, with even more stringent provisions, and appointed a force of state constables. In July, with great fanfaronade, the work of prohibiting the sale of intoxicating drinks began. The reader who is not so fortunate as to live within the bounds of our little but strong State may suppose that this .law was the result of some change in the opinions of the people of Rhode Island ; some deep conviction which gave an impulse to the legislators, and would afford power to enforce and maintain it. A prohibitory law is not made in that way. There was a crisis in Rhode Island politics, worse than

the one which Thackeray so humorously por-
trays in the affairs of England. A senatorial
chair was to be vacated, and the aspirants disputed for the prize. The contest was fierce, with
many ballotings. Mr. X couldn't, Mr. Y
mustn't, and Mr. Z, the temperance leader,
wouldn't come in. The astute managers for
one of the candidates thought that by enacting
a constabulary and prohibitory statute they
could gain a move over their opponents. Mr.
Z, the temperance leader, was personally popular, and might have drawn sufficient support
from the other parties to elect him, but he
wouldn't accept, and in no event could a direct
prohibitionist be elected on that issue; the general government and the United States treasury
have never appreciated prohibition. Therefore
these calculating gentlemen foresaw a prohibitory measure might help their " slate ": thus it
was done. It is whispered about that the men
who actually made this law were not strongly
convinced in their own persons of the good of
total abstinence. It is even hinted that these

politicians do not hold themselves bound by the State law, but remand their allegiance to that higher law which sends taxes on whiskey into the United States treasury, where they are much needed. Besides, those who criticise and carp at these patriots forget that there is no statute in Rhode Island which forbids a legislator or a political manager to drink. The prohibition is upon the *sale.*

The agitators set their machinery in motion during the summer, and in the autumn a lot of cases were under way. It is supposed there are [1] fully five hundred suits instituted. It is evident that, if law and litigation would accomplish the suppression of the traffic, there is enough in process in Rhode Island. They made loud noise, and one might suppose that no man would dare to tap a cask. Still the knowing ones said that the sale was going on in different form, but in as large quantity as ever. The state constables bustled about and worked faithfully as they could; there is no question of their

[1] In December, 1874.

integrity. They could not be entirely fair, as politics are constituted. Where a dealer had strong political influence, — and the shrewd ones among them have this, owing to the inverse working of these very laws, — the constables found it convenient to pass him by. But they seized many stocks of liquors, and large ones, to await trial under the new statute. There is so much good done, you will say; to get any substantial quantity of liquors out of the shops is a blessing. Innocent! you do not understand the plain ways of liquor laws. As soon as the state constable attaches, the dealer puts his legal machinery at work. The ownership of these large stocks of liquors is in men who live in New York. They at once sue, and the United States marshal, one greater than the state constable, takes possession. Well, the liquors are safe, good women will say; some good is done. Not at all. The United States assumes no further responsibility than it is obliged to, in any civil suit, for any property interest. In this suit, it only cares for the plaintiff, who wants his liquor, therefore the marshal appoints a keeper who is satisfactory to the plaintiff, and if he chooses he appoints a clerk of the Rhode Island dealer. The marshal has no other course open to him; he discharges his duty morally and legally when he satisfies the plaintiff. So the liquors have rounded the circumlocution office, and passed back into the virtual control of the dealer from whom they started. The dealer then goes on retailing with a small stock at risk of seizure, but the bulk of his property is under the virtual protection of the United States government. The fault is not in any executive, it is in the law itself, which starts in injustice and ends in absurdity. If you say the same evasion might follow any law of regulation, we answer no. Any law which does not work out public sentiment will be evaded, if not by the above process, by some other equally ingenious. But ingenuity never saved a public offender where the public were in earnest. The public mind assents to the theory of regulation; enthusiasts attempt to turn that sentiment into prohibition; the result in practice is a mush which is neither prohibitory nor regulative.

All this legal and governmental commotion produced a corresponding effect on the public mind. The newspapers were filled with noisy assertions that liquor-dealing was crushed or being crushed, and that prohibition was exalting itself day by day in the estimation of the citizens of Rhode Island. This expression culminated in the testimony of Gov. Howard, who is politically affiliated with the prohibitionists, at a convention of the Rhode Island Temperance Union. He said : —

... " I stopped short without recommending particularly the prohibitory law. I did so because I was not fully convinced that it was the best remedy to be found ; but the law was adopted. After a long time we succeeded in selecting such a force of men as was needed to execute those laws ; and now, ladies and gentlemen, I am here to-night, especially for the purpose of saying, not from the stand-point of a temperance man, but as a public man with a full sense of the responsibility which attaches to me from my representative position, that to-day the prohibitory laws of this State, if not a complete success, are a success beyond the fondest anticipations of any friend of temperance, in my opinion. Ladies and gentlemen, prohibitory legislation in Rhode Island is a success to a marvellous extent. I have desired, I have felt it incumbent upon me to make that declaration, and I desire that it shall go abroad as my solemn assertion."[1]

This was on the eve of the 29th of October. " The Union," the organ of the prohibitory party, on the 4th of December, in an article entitled " The Future Outlook for Prohibition," makes this statement: —

" What has been done to enforce the law, aside from the labors performed by two or three of the seven deputies?[2] Why, little or nothing at all. *The dealers in intoxicating liquors have made some little changes in their mode of doing business, and the business goes forward* just as defiantly as though it were a virtue to trample the statutes of a little State like Rhode Island under foot."

The piteous whine for the little State was gratuitous,. for Massachusetts conflicts in the same or similar processes of law with the gen-

---

1 Extract from report of speech in " Providence Journal."
2 *i.e.,* State constables.   The italics are ours.

eral government. The statement of the " Union"
was correct, and confirmed by the common observation of all except the few whose brains
and ears were filled with prohibitory prejudice.[1]
If the law was a dead or dying failure on the
4th of December, it is obvious that it could not
have been " a marvellous success" on the 29th
of October, only five weeks previous. Gov.
Howard is an honorable man, more unselfish

---

[1] Since the above was in type, Mayor Doyle, of Providence, has published his annual report, and we cite : —
" The number of arrests during the past year has been less
than in the preceding year; and this fact was to have been
expected from the depression of business, particularly in the
manufacturing branches. This result has been observed in
police experience heretofore. At such times the arrests for
drunkenness and small offences growing out of the use of intoxicating liquors decrease. The enactment of a prohibitory
liquor law has not reduced the number of places for the sale of
liquor in this city. At the present time, the number of places
where liquor can be obtained is larger than at any time heretofore. It has, however, changed the mode of selling; and, in
many of the places, instead of a variety of liquors being kept
on hand and in considerable quantity, a single kind and but a
small quantity is now kept where it can be found. There has
been considerable increase during the past few months in the
number of young men upon the streets under the influence of
liquor, and complaints of rowdyism from this class are becom-
ing very frequent, far more so than we have been accustomed
to receive."

than ordinary politicians. The facts prove the political principles we stated in our introduction. An honest man, deluded by the noise of zealots, is driven into a declaration which his common sense would never have entertained, if he could have allowed that wholesome monitor to be heard. It is seldom the futility of prohibition is proven in such dramatic experience, but the principle is the same everywhere. Rhode Island is a small community, and makes history promptly, whether in the Dorr rebellion, the Union struggle, or in the vagaries of prohibition. The law works quickly, the reaction is speedy, and these facts are thrown out upon the surface, so that people must recognize them. The statute is the same as elsewhere, a little more stringent perhaps, it being the latest contrivance; the people are much the same in their habits with those of other Eastern States.

The writer has enjoyed the freest confidence of the officers of the law in almost every department of its administration. He has never found one who believed the law has been or can be executed in such a way as to sensibly lessen the traffic in intoxicating liquors. Many interesting facts coming from their sources have gathered in the writer's note-book while he has been investigating this matter; he has space for but few of them. While the State and the United States officers were trying their strength over the liquor in the barrel, what were the retailers about? To the eye, many shops were dry;[1] but on one street there were fourteen dwellings which had meanwhile begun to retail spirits. Imagine the consequences of converting fourteen homes into drinking dens, — this on one street, — then extend the picture over a large city. These were the haunts of the poorer classes. At the same time, one man had upon his pocket-ring seven keys to as many different club-rooms opened for the purpose of drinking. The upper classes, as they are called, organized these clubs in all quarters of the city; we have already cited evidence showing the

[1] In other cases the sale kept on. There would be three different seizures at one shop within two months. Yet the daily sale would hardly be diminished.

effects of these illicit institutions. The positive effect produced by the law was chiefly in cutting off uses of liquors, which all but extremists would agree were not harmful. This instance occurred, and we give it in the words of one of the parties concerned : —

"A German woman expecting to die desires the communion in conformity with the usages of her church. She sends for a clergyman, who has no wine, in consequence of the prohibitory law. To obtain the wine, the clergyman applied without success to a fellow-clergyman, and then, the matter being urgent, he addressed a note to a respectable druggist, who reluctantly furnishes a small amount of vile stuff. Through a mistake, the wine was sent to the clergyman's house, who could not conscientiously convey this stuff to the patient, and destroyed it. He applied to a leading druggist, knowing him personally, for some pure wine. The druggist most reluctantly furnished the article desired, which was presently forwarded to the patient. The patient, when it arrived, no longer needed the wine, or the communion, or the pastor."

This pathetic story is an exceptional affair, but it truly illustrates the cumbrous working of that legal machinery which, created to catch the virtuous and vicious alike, allows the vicious to slip through, and ensnares the few people whose consciences would need no statute.

The writer was obliged to send to New York at about this time for a jug of cooking wine. He could not get it in Providence without breaking the law,[1] though it was notorious that the law was being broken daily.

The number of persons who are habitually or often drunk, in proportion to the whole number who drink liquors, is not as large as we generally suppose. In the city of Providence, the population of 1873 was, in round numbers, 85,000.

"During the year 1873, in the total number of arrests there were 4,211 different persons, instead of 5,920; there being 1,040 persons previously arrested for the same offence during the year from two to twenty-three times, and is equal to 1,709 arrests; the number of non-residents arrested was 1,140. By deducting these, we have but 3,071 persons arrested for drunkenness that were actual residents of this

---

[1] At that time a few dealers were selling on licenses not expired. But they were not of the class with whom the writer is wont to deal. Neither the grocer nor apothecary could then legally sell a gallon of cooking wine.

city, — the number of *repeaters* being equal to 29 per cent of the total arrests, and the number of non-residents equal to 19 per cent, — making the number of repeaters and non-residents equal to 48 per cent of the whole number. The number of repeaters has gradually decreased during the past four years. This may, to a very great extent, be attributed to the good influences brought to bear through the united labors of the various temperance organizations in the city and state.[1]

Respecting the non-residents, the report says " they were employed in laying water-pipes for the introduction of Pawtuxet water, in building sewers and reservoirs, and in widening streets, &c. I think I am safe in saying that eight-tenths of this number were men of intemperate habits, and a very large proportion of them are classed among the repeaters for the last four years."

If the matter of drinking was confined to these unfortunate wards of the police, it might perhaps be more easily controlled. But look at the facts. In 1872, the police report 22 drug stores selling under license, and 358 other places of sale, making 380. In 1873, there were about as

---

[1] Report of the Chief of Providence Police, p. 15.

many; it is not a question of strict prohibition; the new act did not begin until July, 1874.
These 380 places would furnish a shop for every
12 of the above-named 4,211 common drunkards.
Twelve customers would hardly support a shop,
even if they drank without cessation. Besides,
no traffic was ever sustained by that class of persons exclusively. A traffic so extensive as this
gets a portion of the wages of solid industry,
or it could never sustain its wide proportions.

The writer was able to investigate the drinking habits of a group of 168 adult workingmen.
It was a picked force, common laborers, with a
fair proportion of skilled men. Of these, 68 were
abstinence men, and 100, or about 60 per cent,
drank alcoholic liquors more or less. None of
these were habitual drunkards, and very few
were occasionally intoxicated. These latter
were most affected by the Sunday drinking,
which is the worst form of intemperance.
Hardly any of these men were to be found
among the arrested, resident or non-resident.
A man of this class would lose caste among his
fellows should he be arrested. These are not

"statistics," but actual facts, and other groups of laborers would doubtless afford similar results. The point at issue is not whether it is wise or unwise for these men to drink liquors, but whether society, as a whole, can absolutely prohibit an appetite which fully one-half of the respectable laboring people consider reasonable. Of the habits of the so-called upper classes, the reader can judge for himself.

It is acknowledged that while the legal measures are being pushed, the efforts of the Temples of Honor and other voluntary temperance associations in Rhode Island are lessened, and the corresponding results are less. These associations and all methods of temperance reform need a constant supply of personal enthusiasm, and it is this vital influence which affects the drunkard and forces him to change his habits. Naturally, while the prohibitionists are praying to Hercules, and trying to force the law into impossible channels, the enthusiasm which would find a legitimate exercise upon individuals is absorbed and lost in grinding at the great government mill.

THE GROUNDS OF PROHIBITION.

———◆———

IT may be useful to look toward the grounds on which the prohibitionists rest their arguments, and to consider the subject from their point of view. In 1866 and 1867 a strong petition was made to the Massachusetts legislature for a license law, or for such change in the then prohibitory statute as would recognize the sale of liquors. This petition was supported by Governor Andrew, and a joint special committee devoted long sessions to the hearing of testimony on both sides. Numbers of leading citizens, representing almost every vocation, were examined by one party or the other. Rev. Dr. A. A. Miner, a distinguished Universalist divine, appeared for the Massachusetts Temperance Alliance and the remonstrants, or the supporters of the prohibitory statute. The

remonstrance was strong and weighty, representing generally the influence of " the active
friends of temperance, the tried and true co-
laborers," using the language of their own report. The petition failed.

Dr. Miner's argument[1] lasted three and a
half hours, and fills a pamphlet of 122 pages.
As might be supposed, from the gravity of the
occasion, he gathered all the points relied on by
prohibitionists, and we shall quote freely from
his exposition.   In one sense the argument, as a
whole, supports our main issue, for it is a total
abstinence plea addressed to a majority in a
legislature constituted in the manner we have
described.   As we claim that legislation must
ground itself on the actual life of the whole
people, and not on the moral desires of a faction,
however worthy that desire may be, it is a strong
collateral proof of our position, that the prohibitionists must argue teetotally and not generally.

To get the drift of the argument, we will

[1] Argument on the Right and Duty of Prohibition. A. A.
Miner. Boston : Wright & Potter, Printers.

state, briefly and clearly as we can, the points
which he makes, some by proof and some by
assertion, in the order in which they stand : —

— The agitation is a liquor-dealer's movement.

— Teetotalism is the only temperance — and better than any use of liquors.

— A strong array of statistics, showing the material cost and increase of disease by intemperance ;
also the indirect cost through crime.

— " Alcohol is classed as a poison." [1] This assertion is nowhere established. There is much contra-
dictory testimony discussed on respiratory food,
and especially whether " alcohol is assimilative, that
it does the office of food by arresting the disintegra-
tion of tissues." The weight of testimony cited by
the Doctor bears toward this latter view, but he
claims the opposite. He keeps to his direct statement that it is poison, though he does not bring
sufficient proof. [2]

— The general inutility of alcoholic beverages is
established through Dr. Carpenter.

[1] Argument, p. 44.

[2] Dr. Miner relies much on the statement of " the elder Dr.
Bigelow, that if intoxicating beverages had never been discovered, the well-being of the race would have been promoted."
The writer respectfully suggests to both the reverend and the
medical gentlemen, that is one of the mysterious things " no
feller can find out."

— There is less drunkenness ·in Massachusetts than in wine-drinking countries.

— "There is not the slightest evidence of the Scriptures giving any countenance whatever to the use of fermented liquors."[1] " Paul was a total abstainer, Timothy was a total abstainer."[2]

— Liquors may be useful as medicines, but not as beverages; even if useful as beverages, social example requires abstinence.

— Disputes Stuart Mill's position, that drinking is a right of individual liberty; claiming that the social right of restraint is equivalent to right to suppress obscene books, or to restrain truancy, and tax for education of the truants. He shows no direct argument for the legal right of prohibition, but claims the right negatively.[3]

— Answering an argument that the law is not executed in Boston, he makes three points:—I. The authorities are to blame therefor. II. It is executed.

[1] Argument, p. 66.
[2] Argument, p. 71.
[3] We cite from page 82 : — " Few, if any, witnesses here have pointedly denied the right of the government to maintain a prohibitory law. Perhaps ex-Governor Clifford is an exception to this remark. When asked if such an enactment does not transcend the legitimate authority of the State, he answered, ' undoubtedly.' At the same time, he proceeded to say that the State has a right to enact laws which, without attempting the impossible, shall restrain the sale and use of intoxicating beverages."

III. The same amount of non-execution would exist
under a license law.

— Public opinion sustains prohibition.

— That under the state constabulary the traffic
and drunkenness in Boston both diminished in two
months.

— That club-rooms spring up, but they need
not.

— Desire for social excitement, claimed as inherent,
is actually promoted by drinking usages, and is artificial, to be cured by rearing several generations free
from drinking usage.

— Natural obstinacy excited by prohibitory law
" applies to every criminal law and to every criminal
act as well as to this."

— The grand democracy of our institutions can
suppress the traffic, though the old world fails.[1]

— Discretion should not be given towns nor cities.
License is a reversal of prohibition. " Everywhere
rich voluptuaries will combine with imbruted ignorance to bear down the sober industry of the commonwealth." [2] " If I were to define a license law,
stringent or otherwise, engrafted upon our present
law or standing alone, I would say that it is a legal
means of recruiting the army of drunkards with the
approbation of ex-governors of the commonwealth,

---

[1] Argument, p. 104.   [2] Argument, p. 107.

whiskey-drinking priests, and members of the Faculty of Harvard Medical College." [1]

— Respectable traffic is impossible. " Massachusetts cannot enact a law that will make the selling of liquors respectable. If the angel Gabriel should come down to earth and sell liquors as beverages, he would not lift the business up to heaven, but the business would drag the angel down to hell." [2]

— Alleged duplicity of temperance men retorted on " moderate indulgers." " Take the quantity and the quality of the liquors adulterated ; take the tergiversations, subterfuges, and evasions of those who say they will obey the law and do not ; take all these into account, and we have duplicity, and enough of it. Remember that here is a foe to be watched, to be guarded ; and if you have a stronghold on this enemy, in the name of righteousness and of good order, I exhort you not to let go that hold." [3]

The writer solemnly affirms, as the Friend would say, that in drawing out this analysis he did not mean to make the points turn against the argument. Not every point made is quoted in detail, — our space would not allow it, — but

[1] Argument, p. 110.   [2] Argument, p. 110.
[3] Argument, p. 120.

every strong one is stated, and as fairly as we
are able.

Dr. Miner is an able contestant, and a man
of high moral standing. He would not use
these same arguments, and in the manner he
uses them, before the Supreme Court, nor before
a jury of his peers, men of intelligence equal to
his own; he knows cause and effect too well.
He spoke representatively to the Joneses elected
as we indicated, to the galleries, and to the devoted but unreasoning pressure behind. He
knew their prejudices, and he carried his men
with him, defeating John A. Andrew, who was
one of the few American politicians with a
statesmanlike comprehension. No man yet ever
questioned the sincerity of his character.

There is no difference of opinion between
Andrew, Miner, or the writer on intemperance,
the evils of intemperance, and the desirability
of limiting drink and the facilities for drinking
to the lowest minimum society will undertake
in good faith and maintain effectually. The
difference is, that some of us think there is such

5*

a thing as temperance in the use of liquors; that
the habits of society show this, and that it ought
to be recognized positively in the law ; that the
law should make legal what is a gross and open
matter of fact, that the illegality should be confined to abuse in drinking, and to criminal abuse
of the drinker, by the seller or by anybody else.
Now these differences of opinion are based on
facts, or they are not. If they are difference
of fact, no amount of screaming at an unchris-
tian and immoral world, no calling of persons by
hard names, will overcome the difference.

If teetotalism is the only moral basis; if spirituous and fermented liquors are poisons, like
strychnine and arsenic ; if sober industry never
drinks ; if to drink at all is unscriptural and un-
christian ; if the great majority of Massachusetts
people, in view of such plain truths, had made
up their minds not to drink at all, why, in the
name of reason, did not such a moral power
show itself in the daily average life of the
people of the State ?

If only " rich voluptuaries," " imbruted ig-

norance." and a few "godly men in error"
were on the wrong side of this question, what
causes can explain the enormous differences of
social opinion and social action in the matter?
An argument of this sort must sustain itself on
all sides, or it topples over the sooner for the
extra weight on one side. If these assertions
were all proofs, and the proofs had their foundation in facts, just as they occur ; that is, in the
facts of common sense and common experience,
then the statute would work itself out as simply
as the law against stealing. According to the
Doctor's theory, and to frequent statements of
abstinence politicians, the whole country portion
of Massachusetts is reduced to strict temperance under the operation of the law. Only
Boston and a few districts in the largest towns
dare to sell any liquors under these prohibitory
statutes, they say. " The valuation of Boston
is stated by Hon. Otis Clapp at $415,000,000,
and the liquor interest at $40,000,000. John
Glancy (who he is I don't know), at the liquor-
dealers' meeting, placed the sum at $90,000,000

to $100,000,000. I think the valuation con-
firms the last statement." [1] If only the consoli-
dated wealth, " ex-governors," and the lowest
orders of society have any interest in the sale
of liquors, how is this immense sum employed?
Are fifty to one hundred millions of capital
briskly occupied in pouring liquors into Boston,
with the few large centres noticed and the
small reservoirs in Vermont and New Hamp-
shire, where similar laws prevail? Connecticut
and Rhode Island draw their supplies from New
York; and Maine must be left out of the account, for have we not been assured that she is
completely converted and sobered under the
blessings of her own original law? Verily, there
is less "sober industry" in Massachusetts than
we had all supposed, or else this sober element
of society sometimes drinks, and helps to employ
this large aggregation of capital,— a kind of
capital which turns itself faster than any other
in commerce, and makes the quickest possible
returns of traffic.

[1] Argument, p. 77.

Boston transacts a large business of all sorts; and here it is shown that more than ten per cent of her whole property is employed in a traffic which, according to prohibitory advocates, is carried on with the outlaws and criminals of society, men who have no rights under the law. Evidently there is a mistake somewhere, and, as we think, it lies in this wilful perversion of the facts. Good men exhaust their moral energy in obtaining impracticable statutes, and then shut their eyes to the plain fact that they are broken at every corner. At best they institute temporary spurts of prohibitory energy, which drive the corner-breakers into secret retreats until the overstrained energies of the prosecutors relax, when they come out into daylight again. These figures prove the position taken in our next chapter, viz., that one strong feature of these statutes as law is, that they are so easily broken. Fifty to one hundred millions of capital are accumulated; and the observation of a child for any period of six months proves that this sum is not idle.

The possessors of this immense force are satisfied in its profitable employment, or they would not keep in the same traffic, turning hither and thither with new expedients as the legislators and prosecutors devise new methods in pursuit. Just as the hare doubles away from his pursuers, except that the pursuing law goes with soft and easy feet, while the escaping liquor-seller has the sharp teeth and desperate grasp of the hound. We complain of their rapacious character as a class. When and where were outlaws other than rapacious, and who makes these men into outlaws?

Those who think unwise laws can be sustained by the moral sense alone should consider the old revenue laws of England. These statutes grew weaker and weaker in enforcement until nearly all the brandies, silks, and other articles of high value were smuggled from the continent, and freely hawked about the streets of London at such prices that every one could see the fact. The evil grew into such proportions that a Whig leader, making

a speech on revenue laws, drew an illicit pon-
gee from his pocket, flourished it, like a flag
of defiance, over the house of commons, and
absolutely blew his nose in the face of the
law-makers of the realm. It was the signal
for the death of the unwise system; and well-
adjusted duties soon sent the silk handkerchiefs
through the customs and the smugglers into
honest industry. Did the Whig statesman
break the law? Technically, we must allow
that he did; but in the better use of law and
statesmanship he did right when he showed
in open daylight the shams of society and the
inconsistency of the law.

We must invite notice just here to some
remarks of De Tocqueville on the influences
which help " to mitigate that tyranny of the
majority " which he dreaded: —

"It must not, moreover, be supposed that the
legal spirit is confined, in the United States, to
the courts of justice; it extends far beyond them.
. . . The Americans, who have made so many
innovations in their political laws, have introduced

very sparing alterations in their civil laws, and
that with great difficulty, although many of these
laws are repugnant to their social condition. The
reason of this is, that, in matters of civil law,
the majority are obliged to defer to the authority
of the legal profession; and the American lawyers are disinclined to innovate when left to their
own choice. . . . Their (*i.e.*, the judges') influence
extends far beyond the limits of the courts; in
the recreations of private life as well as in the
turmoil of public business, in public and in the
legislative assemblies, the American judge is constantly surrounded by men, who are accustomed
to regard his intelligence as superior to their
own." — *Democracy in America*, I., 357, 366.

We should hardly expect the prohibitory
law-makers to take this high view of the office
and influence of lawyers. As a class, they
do not recognize the proper province of this
profession, looking on it as a sort of necessary
evil, and not a natural outgrowth of civilization. Civil life has produced law and lawyers, and they are bulwarks of liberty as well
as of good morals. We should expect that in
arguing for a law the prohibitory men would

produce all the legal authority they could muster; accordingly, we looked for some absolute opinion that the prohibitory statutes are good law through and through ; but, as stated in the analysis, we failed to discover it. They had eminent lawyers on the stand, but could only get such semi-patriarchal, semi-legal expressions as these: " If the prohibitory law could be executed so as entirely to suppress drunkenness, without any evil to the community from the absence of the means of drunkenness," he was " not prepared to say that a prohibitory law might not be a subject of legislation, without regarding the sale and use of intoxicating beverages as especially sinful." — *Hon. Joel Parker.*[1]

Hon. Emory Washburn would " sustain the present law and prohibit the sale of liquor if he could ; and if it should be carried out, he would go the whole length of the matter."[2]

None of these learned and wise men would

[1] Miner, Argument, p. 83. [2] Argument, p. 84.

say the law is good law, though they evidently meant to throw their social influence on the side of temperance, and even of prohibition, if this could be made practicable. They were waiting, in the same posture the courts of law were in, until society should show itself in earnest either to stop drinking and selling liquors or else to give up an impossible undertaking. No one who has studied social development and social law supposes the question will remain in such perplexing doubt for all time.

To understand the guarded statements of these lawyers, we must consider the nature of the statutes themselves: —

"The seizure clause, Judge Sanger says, is the most efficient instrumentality of the law, and with which there is no difficulty whatever in the execution of the law. Whether the jury agree or disagree, the liquors are held, in which case they are practically confiscated; and if the dealer lays in another stock, that stock may also be seized." [1]

This would be cool talk for the emperor of

---

[1] Argument, p. 87.

all the Russias to utter, whatever people may
think of it in this latitude. But these New
England States maintain the strongest government the world has ever known : it can stand a
great deal of imprudence and unwisdom. The
lawyers do not hold that arbitrary power can
never be exercised for social purposes. It is one
of the nice questions of social order when it is
to be exercised, and then it must be used in the
least possible amount ; above all, it must be effective. A captain is allowed to cut away his
mast only in extreme peril, and because it is
an aggravation of the immediate danger. He
proceeds at once to replace it. The institutions
these arbitrary statutes endanger, viz., the right
of property, trial by jury, pure testimony, general respect for law, &c., are to society as the
masts and rigging are to a ship. To attempt to
run good morals by breaking or impairing these,
is as wise and proves to be as effective as it
would be to sail a ship into safety by cutting
away masts and supports.

It is worth while to cite from Mill the statement of the Secretary of the British Temperance Alliance in his letter to Lord Stanley : —

"If any thing invades my social rights, certainly the traffic in strong drink does. It destroys my primary right of security, by constantly creating and stimulating social disorder. It invades my right of equality, by deriving a profit from the creation of a misery I am taxed to support. It impedes my right to free moral and intellectual development, by surrounding my path with dangers,[1] and by weakening and demoralizing society, from which I have a right to claim mutual aid and intercourse."

Mill replies : —

"A theory of social rights, the like of which probably never found its way into distinct language, — being nothing short of this, that it is the absolute social right of every individual that every other individual shall act in every respect exactly as he

---

[1] We believe if the abstinence reformers, to whose noble qualities we have paid grateful respect, only had a little sense of the humorous, they would see the fatal inconsistency of many of their positions and efforts. This proposterous issue can only be met by a joke. The writer has a weakness for warm stewed lobsters at supper, yet he is pretty sure of a nightmare if he indulges the appetite. Now, if we should gravely undertake a crusade against the lobster-dealer for surrounding our path with dangers, &c., would it not be funny?

ought ; that whosoever fails thereof in the smallest particular violates my social right, and entitles me to demand from the legislature the removal of the grievance. So monstrous a principle is far more dangerous than any single interference with liberty : there is no violation of liberty which it would not justify."

It is hardly worth while to discuss Miner's counter-argument, that as truant children are restrained and educated, obscene books prohibited, &c., so social rights are established, and liberty restrained at the will of society. Minds which can see no difference between truancy and the right of an individual to drink, with a consequent right to purchase liquors, will legislate blindly ; they will not stop at distinctions. Mr. Mill and the secretary embody some of the most important social issues in their two statements, and the writer can add nothing to the complete refutation the philosopher gives the reformer. People who think with the secretary look on a statute, having a good moral intention once established by a majority vote, as having the same force as a law of God ; no matter how it is executed, if the intention of the makers was good, then the statute is a part of the great moral scheme of the Almighty government. This applies to social and moral law much the same principle which the Roman ecclesiastics *executed* upon Copernicus with his physical laws. As the statutes of the church were established, then it was a law of God that the solar system could not move. As Mill indicates, the province of law is to work out ordinary social life with least oppression to the individual. Perfect government is for God alone, and God's laws, whatever be the theory of their transmission, establish themselves in the human soul through means of their own — that is, in kind, — and not by mere majority votes.

While we are treating with the prohibitionists on· their own grounds, let us consider their methods of administration : —

"Mr. Frank Edson, agent of the town of Hadley, testified that liquor-drinking was on the increase, and that clubs had sprung up in neighboring towns, instancing Northampton. It appeared, on cross-examination, that he was not a total abstainer, that he had joined one of the objectionable clubs at Northampton, and that liquors were drank in that club. I submit that such testimony is not competent. I believe that men who come up here and set forth the evils which they allege grow out of the law, and then turn around and confess that they are aiding and abetting the breaking of the law themselves, are witnesses whose testimony should be received with great caution." [1]

The point Dr. Miner has under consideration is matter of fact, as to whether there are clubs or not. It was notorious that such clubs grew up wherever the law was actually enforced. Now, any legal or governmental expert would hold that frank testimony like the above should be welcomed in any practical issue of government. A man who was manly enough to confess his own knowledge of such evil practices would, under most social systems, be encouraged if he was telling the truth. The point to be ascertained was whether the law made temptations which hurt the "public welfare," as

[1] Argument, 100.

Paley has it. If no one could tell the truth but
a man who totally abstained, then society was
at low ebb, for those were few, as we have
shown. Few persons would treat their own
sons in this way, if they were bearing testimony
as to the working of laws the parents had set
over them. Probably the Joneses elected by
coalitions took heed and "spotted" all the Ed-
sons and similar men; but was the town of
Hadley, though it might receive a new liquor
agent, benefited by this snubbing of a man who
tried to tell the truth?

We have dwelt upon this point, because it
illustrates much of the prohibitory method both
in argument and in practical administration.

PROHIBITION AND REGULATION.

T HE use of liquors should be regulated and the abuse prevented so far as possible. The traffic is dangerous, but is none the less necessary. The prohibitionists have always treated their various statutes, forbidding the sale of alcoholic liquors, as if they were mere rules for the good order of society. All societies make laws to promote the health of their peoples, and to stop nuisances or hurtful influences. No society or legislature has ever declared alcoholic liquors to be absolutely hurtful, nor has gone so far as to make the use and sale of liquors a nuisance in theoretical principle. This course would have brought the reformers against the rocks of positive law, and they must take another direction. Accordingly, they admit the sale

6

under certain narrow restrictions, which must
save the whole process from its conflict with positive law.   Then they proceed to cut off the sale
of liquors as beverages, without establishing the
fact that they are not beverages[1] legally considered.   In view of the facts of experience, and
of the common habits of the society legislated
for, is this in any fair sense a regulation of a
traffic ?

In debating the true meaning of a law or
a custom, it is well to look into the words
themselves which divide the issues.   Words
are more than names; they are the moulds
into which fluid ideas cast themselves.   When
the idea decays, the word is either dropped
out of use or becomes the ready-made shell
for another idea kindred to it.   Webster and
Worcester define the word "prohibition" in
terms nearly identical, — "An interdiction ; a
forbiddance."   They both quote in exposition

---

[1] " That spirituous and intoxicating liquors were still property, notwithstanding this act (Maine Law in Rhode Island),
is certain."— *B. R. Curtis, Circuit Court Reports*, p. 828.

from Tillotson, viz.: "The law of God in the
Ten Commandments consists mostly of *pro-
hibitions;* thou shalt not do such a thing."
Let us look at the synonyms for regulate.
"To direct, as applied to the administration
of affairs, is more authoritative than to conduct, while conduct is more active or oper-
ative. Regulate stands midway between."[1]
Is there any actual correspondence or kindred
agreement between these two terms? The
first word embodies the power of direct, positive law, that portion of it which lies deepest
in us. "The whole or a portion of the laws
set by God to men is frequently styled the
law of nature, or natural law; being, in
truth, the only natural law of which it is
possible to speak without a metaphor, or
without a blending of objects which ought
to be distinguished broadly. But, rejecting
the appellation 'law of nature' as ambig-
uous and misleading, I name those laws or
rules, as considered collectively or in a mass,

[1] Synonyms Discriminated. By C. J. Smith.

the *Divine law*, or the *law of God*."[1]   There is
the root of prohibition, which old Tillotson
found out; the tables of stone brought these
strong bonds of order down to us; let any
legislator beware of trifling with these divine
laws.

A statute, in order to base itself on this
strong and divine foundation, should carry
with it the imperative moral sense, the overwhelming accord of the society enacting it,
and at the time of its enactment. We might
draw many interesting illustrations from the
history of American slavery, but let us take
simpler experience. Suppose a village owned
a public square, around which some of the
villagers wished to play base ball. Before
any statute could be made, a very large
majority must agree whether they would play
ball at all. If there was a public discussion to settle the principles of ball playing,
as to whether a ball properly made, properly handled, would or would not break the

1 Austin's Jurisprudence.   Ed. 1873.   I. 88.

windows exposed, would or would not break the thumbs of players, would or would not break the heads of little boys, the results could not be embodied in a statute until certain definite principles were settled. Before they could regulate ball playing so that the minority would not be oppressed, society as a whole, not a mere majority, must decide the main question whether they would play ball at all, where the public had common rights. A statute to police the operation would effect little while property-owners had rights which the discussion could not touch. This is an illustration, and not a parallel. Balls do not mean whiskey, nor bats the clubs which ruffians use to knock over temperance law-makers; we are only trying to make the above statement clear.

Again; hardly any sane person would think of making a statute at this day to stop the sale of playing-cards, whatever his own opinion of cards might be. He might regulate the sale by any restriction utility might

demand. He would forbid their sale to mi-
nors, or sale for use in gambling, or undertake any such method which could be
established judiciously. But fifty to one hundred years ago, in New England, a law prohibiting the sale would have found ready
obedience. Playing-cards have not changed,
nor has New England lost its reverence for
law meanwhile. But the attitude of society
toward amusements has changed largely. To
the old Puritan, any game of chance was an
offence against the law of God; he would prohibit cards totally. Playing-cards in the modern
view (which sustains a statute against gambling) carry with them elements of evil, yet
society will not cut itself off from their use
because gamblers abuse them.

These prohibitory statutes can have only one
place in the system of civilized law: this system
divides itself into three classes: —

"The first comprises the laws (properly so ·
called) which are set by God to his human creatures.

" The second comprises the laws (properly so called) which are set by men as political superiors, or by men, as private persons in pursuance of legal rights.

" The third comprises laws of the two following species : 1. The laws (properly so called) which are set by men to men, but not by men as political superiors, nor by men as private persons, in pursuance of legal rights. 2. The laws which are closely analogous to laws proper, but are merely opinions or sentiments held or felt by men in regard to human conduct.

" I name laws of the first class the *law* or *laws of God*, or *the Divine law* or *laws.*

" For various reasons, which I shall produce immediately, I name laws of the second class *positive law*, or *positive laws.*

" For the same reasons, I name laws of the third class *positive morality, rules of positive morality*, or *positive moral rules.* . . .

" The name *morality*, when standing unqualified or alone, may signify the human laws, which I style positive morality, as considered without reference to their goodness or badness."[1]

These liquor statutes fall under the second division of the third class: they are analogous to laws proper, but are merely legal formulas for carrying into effect the opinions or sentiments held or felt by men in regard to human conduct. Or, as we said on another occasion, they formulate the sentimental consciousness of the majority into a statute which shall attempt to make morals for the minority.

Mr. Austin[2] does not state, nor do we mean to claim through him, that a statute under this class is necessarily bad law. We admit that if the great mass of society were totally abstinent, a statute against the sale of liquor as a beverage might be maintained as an administrative expedient. There would then be an efficient "sanction" of the law, as the jurists' term

[1] Austin's Jurisprudence, I. pp. 174–176.

[2] We believe the authority of Austin is not disputed in the main principles of jurisprudence. John Stuart Mill says of him : "He accomplished through life little in comparison with what he seemed capable of; but what he did produce is held in the very highest estimation by the most competent judges."

runs.[1] The fact that it would be so easily maintained would almost make it unnecessary. We
do not need a statute against killing to quicken
our moral sense of crime. We need it to catch
the murderer, and hang or imprison him. The
sanction of the law is anterior to it, and is not
created by it. If people, or the great majority
of people, did not desire to drink, then it would
be easy to control the selling of liquor. Prohibition or regulation would then adjust itself to
the positive morality of the law, which would
become moral in the true sense, in that it would
embody the best conviction of society. But
to make the seller a criminal while the drinker
commits no crime in drinking, is a legal absurdity, which the common sense of the community
has detected, as their average conduct shows.
Compare Burke, III. 319 : —

[1] " The object of this law does not appear to be so much
' for the suppression of drinking-houses and tippling-shops,' as
its title would seem to import, as for the destruction of intoxicating liquors — because they may be injurious to the community. The main principle of all these statutes is the same.
The later ones are changed only in details." — *Curtis, Circuit
Court Reports,* p. 337.

"No other given part of legislative rights can be exercised, without regard to the general opinion of those who are to be governed. That general opinion is the vehicle and organ of legislative omnipotence. Without this, it may be a theory to entertain the mind, but it is nothing in the direction of affairs. . . In effect, to follow, not to force, the public inclination; to give a direction, a form, a technical dress, and a specific sanction to the general sense of the community, is the true end of legislature."

Failing in this moral sanction, the prohibitionists substitute the pressure of a majority vote, and the feeling which the evils of intemperance always excite in any humane person. Now, both these principles are powerful in their legitimate sphere, but neither one can enforce a statute law unless it be sustained by other powerful influences, which combined, make up even justice. Here is an appetite which is common, nay, well-nigh universal. Stimulants are used from the poles to the equator, — a fungus in Siberia; betel and bhang or hemp in Asia; ava in Polynesia; fermented mare's milk in Russia, where it is too cold for vegetable fer-

mentations; maté in South America; coca leaf
in Peru; tea, coffee, tobacco, opium, alcoholic
and fermented liquors in all quarters of the
earth: all these attest a desire, a craving for
stimulants, which is more than cosmopolitan;
it is human. A portion of the people in one
country assert that this desire is injudicious and
harmful. They prohibit all sale of alcoholic
stimulants, articles desired by the larger half
of the community, because, as they say, the
state should not allow rumsellers to make paupers and criminals. The evidence is no more
certain that, a pauper or criminal will be made
when a man buys a glass of beer or whiskey,
than it is certain when a person buys a rope
that he will hang himself. Neither a majority
vote nor a moral sentiment will change this
essential principle, and make the gratification
of a natural appetite into a crime against the
state. There are two courses open to the moralists. Either remove the desire from individuals, or take control of the traffic and gratify
the desire in its minimum. Imperial or Papal

Rome themselves could not make a third course possible. If the legal traffic is absolutely suppressed while the appetite remains, it merely runs into illicit channels, as we have shown.

An absolute proof of the exceptional and unnatural character of prohibition is afforded by its success in those rare cases where it has succeeded. For example, during the great Boston fire it was easy to close all liquor shops and stop the sale effectively for some days. This was a despotic measure, made reasonable by the extraordinary occasion; therefore everybody, sellers and drinkers, generally acquiesced. "In the midst of arms the laws are dumb." Law, in its nature, must be fitted to the common living of the people.

"Yet, though hot waters be good to be given to one in a swound, they will burn his heart out who drinks them constantly when in health. Extraordinary courses are not ordinarily to be used, but when enforced by absolute necessity." — FULLER's *Holy State.*

As men are constituted to-day, as the principles of civilized law are to-day, the point at issue is, has a person a right, under the law, to drink a glass or a teaspoonful of alcoholic liquor? If he has that right, he has a right to buy it, and if the state interferes to regulate the natural traffic, it is bound to furnish reasonable means for the gratification of the buyer's desire.

If a man offended against the law of God in drinking, then we could readily bring the seller under one of the great divisions of positive law stated above. We are aware a few abstinents take ground that drinking is an absolute infraction of God's laws, *i.e.*, by interpretation of Scripture. Let them prove it, and the liquor statutes will mend themselves very quickly.

To aggravate the results of contingent crimes does not raise the tone of the community either morally or according to positive moral law. To maintain the moral tone of society in England, only a short time since, they thought it necessary to transport a petty thief, or even to put him to death.[1] The practical result was,

---

[1] It was not until 1811 that Romilly procured the repeal of

that there were more and worse hardened criminals; society was not bettered thereby. This is merely an evidence of the bad working of moral principles in unwise laws. By constructively making an artificial criminal out of the liquor-dealer, we have made these sellers into a hard set morally; we have not helped society, nor the positive morality of the law.

If these things be so, the reader naturally asks how could the laws be enacted or how sustained? In our introductory statement we sketched the process by which a legislature is made, embodying the public sentiment which creates these statutes. A majority is thus constructed out of heterogeneous and inconsistent elements. We have seen its method of working and the results it produces in liquor statutes. To comprehend the dangerous power of this

these cruel statutes; then Lord Ellenborough opposed. " Stealing privately in a shop goods to the value of five shillings or in a dwelling to the value of forty shillings were capital felonies." Likewise they repealed " the ridiculously bloody enactment of Elizabeth, which made it a capital offence in soldiers and marines to be found wandering about the realm without a pass."

majority, let us heed the words of that saga-
cious and friendly observer, De Tocqueville : —

" When an individual or a party is wronged in
the United States, to whom can he apply for re-
dress ? If to public opinion, public opinion constitutes the majority ; if to the legislature, it represents
the majority, and implicitly obeys it ; if to the executive power, it is appointed by the majority, and
serves as a passive tool in its hands. The public
force consists of the majority under arms ; the jury
is the majority invested with the right of hearing
judicial cases ; and in certain States even the judges
are elected by the majority." . . .

" The majority possesses a power which is physical and moral at the same time, which acts upon the
will as much as upon the actions, and represses not
only all contest but all controversy." [1]

A power thus constituted makes a statute,
bringing the whole power of civil government,
with the weapons of arbitrary search and seizure,
to force the common people to stop buying
liquors for beverages. Arbitrary prohibition, to
exist with free institutions, must be enforced
in the common living of freemen, else there is

[1] Democracy in America, I. 332, 337.

tyranny of one portion of the people over another portion. When Mr. Seward's "little bell tinkled," every thoughtful person shuddered, yet he thought that our political life was in imminent peril, and he submitted to this arbitrary stretch of power. Had Mr. Seward used this privilege in any police service or matter of regulation, in any way except for the very salvation of national political life, he would himself have been "tinkled" into Fort Warren.

A statute, before it becomes assured law, must pass through the lower and higher courts. They consider whether it is prohibited under the constitution, or whether it conflicts with other provisions of constitutional law already established. Finally, they consider it in the light of the great principles of reason and justice which underlie all law. In fact, these liquor statutes have never been subjected to this crucial test. The waves of moral sentiment have driven the statutes forward from point to point, in the manner De Tocqueville shows the majority have power to do. One of the best features of civilized law in Anglo-Saxon communities is in its ability to adjust itself to the growing life of the people. The courts, rigid and formal as they are, sympathize with popular feeling, and reflect it faintly in their conduct. This was illustrated in the history of American slavery; the courts gradually swayed about until they made into law the political action of the people. Slavery never seemed so strong as when it had the supreme court in its influence, and had established its arbitrary statutes under the law. It was the recoil from this tyranny over a free nation which sent people, courts, and government into a war for its destruction. The courts have never passed on the essential features of these arbitrary statutes. They have been disposed to push the policing power of the law to its extreme limit, in order to give play to the sentiment and power of the majority in its desire to suppress intemperance. The great principles of positive law have never yet been fully applied to a liquor statute.

Many partial and unjust laws stand on a like

insecure basis. The freedom from taxation of church property, for example, is believed by good authority to be unconstitutional. The matter has never been tried. When the early meeting-houses were built, that seemed the easiest and simplest mode of establishing public worship. Gradually, in our complex civilization, it is growing into grave abuse. Probably, as it grows worse, it will antagonize public opinion until the courts feel the pressure and abolish the evil.

Besides, as we have shown, the readiness to be violated which was inherent in these prohibitory statutes gave them an elasticity of resistance they would not have had if better executed. The lesions and breaks they constantly received made the natural legal resistance less violent. Why resist in the courts a law which was so easily broken in detail? Few liquor-dealers would pay tens of thousands of dollars to obtain a legal privilege of selling when they were making hundreds of thousands by selling illicitly.

" It is of great importance in a republic not only to guard the society against the oppression of its rulers, but to guard one part of society against the injustice of the other part. Justice is the end of government; it is the end of civil society." [1]

Jefferson said: " The executive power in our government is not the only, perhaps not even the principal, object of my solicitude. The tyranny of the legislature is really the danger most to be feared, and will continue to be so for many years to come."

These are not the shrieks of alarmists, but the grave opinions of men who knew the organization of this American society. In view of this imperial power of the majority, with its liability to abuse, it behooves us as citizens to consider the exact relations of the majority to every statute which they enact.

In the early portion of this chapter we remarked that a prohibitory and penal statute should bring to its execution the overwhelming accord of society. Perhaps our thought would be stronger if we should say natural accord. Nature uses two forces mainly in her

[1] Federalist, 51, Jas. Madison.

operations on our earth. One is the power
of weight, we call gravitation, and the other
is the power of growth, we call vital force.
A gardener lately contrived ingenious apparatus by which he made a growing squash lift
over two tons of weight. The simple weight
of the vegetable might be a hundred pounds.
It is this vital power of truth and justice
which gives natural force to the decrees of
a legislature. The majority can sit down with
its weight wherever it pleases; it can gain vital
success for its decrees only when it adjusts
them to the great natural laws ingrained in
the nature of man himself.

Law must be considered not in the light
of theory, but of common usage. Putting
out of the account the criminal classes and
habitual drunkards, we would ask the reader
what proportion of his friends abstain from alcoholic liquors. We mean by abstention, that
it be in practice absolute. You may apply the
medicinal limit at one point, your neighbor at
another; but the expression "total abstinence"

and its correlative " prohibition " are as strong as language can make them. The writer has seen decent people in a good many sections of New England, and he has never yet found a community where one person in every three abstained absolutely. Now, we have shown that prohibition is not regulation; that it has been maintained in abeyance by the legal authority, while the moral force of society might work out the habits and ordinary living on which any sumptuary statute must base itself. If this change of living comes not, then the statutes are tyrannical. It is hard for an American, wrapped in party toils, hampered by caucuses, and governed by politicians, to comprehend that he may be the innocent cause of a tyranny such as Madison so forcibly describes. Yet the writer believes that all of us are implicated, as he will try to show.

The liquor statutes, viewed in a large sense, are laws for sellers and drinkers both, — for you and for me. Every law must have an effective " sanction."

" 'Command ' and ' duty ' are, therefore, correlative terms. . . . The evil which will probably
be incurred in case a command be disobeyed,
or (to use an equivalent expression) in case
a duty be broken, is frequently called a *sanction*, or an *enforcement of obedience*, . . . a
punishment. But as punishments, strictly so
called, are only a *class* of sanctions, the term is
too narrow to express the meaning adequately." [1]
The " sanction, of the law against stealing is
not merely penal and criminal, it is in our ab-
horrence of the moral wrong. Now, when we
vote laws on these moral issues, from the various
motives stated in the foregoing, party pressure,
moral uneasiness, social bearing, &c., we do not
consider this grand principle of sanction which
should first inspire our conduct, or our civic
attitude, as we have called it. We forget that
every right carries with it a corresponding duty,
we speak of right legally. When you enact
that one class of persons shall carry out a certain law, you thereby enlarge the right of these,

[1] Austin, Jurisprudence, I. 92.

and you obligate another class by a duty.[1] The
law officers must execute; all others comprehended must obey. Now, the strange mist in
our minds has befogged the notions of temperates in this regard. A moral right is essential
and sacred, born of the divine within; a legal
right is a constructive and technical thing, by
which society administers order and justice.
While it lasts, it is strong as gravitation itself
in an Anglo-Saxon community. The slave
Burns was driven back into slavery under the
power of the State of Massachusetts, though
three-quarters of her freemen would have killed
every man who laid a hand on him, if simple
murder had been the only crime involved.

The use of liquor runs so easily into passionate abuse, that every man touches it nervously.
Above all, sensitive persons dread the influence
of their acts upon others. All this we formulate
at the polls into a legal right to restrain the
sale of the dreaded stuff; the legal duty which

---

[1] " Rights and obligations, though distinct and opposite in
their nature, are simultaneous in their origin, and inseparable
in their existence." — *Bentham's Theory of Legislation*, p. 93.

should follow we do not propose to ourselves, but lay it upon others. Every temperate man voting prohibition all these years has not prohibited himself thereby, — he has meant to prohibit somebody else. The sale and use of liquors prove this. The temperate see a drunkard in the gutter, an orphan in the asylum, a whiskey-dealer wallowing in his gains; they transmute this moral sensibility into a legal right of prohibition. This legal right thus becomes a tyranny, for there is no corresponding change in the habits of the majority or of the whole public. As said above, the legal right is imposed by the majority, who must always include the temperates : the legal duty, the function of obedience, is laid on a minority. The consequence is the same which has proceeded from all tyrannies, — lying, fraud, plunder, and suborning of testimony. These things have been done by good men with good intentions, but a moral purpose cannot sustain a legal right or power, unless that right symbolizes the actual conduct of the people, and not their maudlin sensibilities.

One essential cause of the weakness of these statutes in their practical application is to be found in the indirection, which is in their conception and intention. They are made to stop the sale of liquors. Why? Because the sale is wrong. Why is it wrong? Because people drink them, and great harm ensues. Is it wrong to drink liquors? Here not one person in ten could give an affirmative answer. No body of legislators or voters has ever said or believed that it is absolutely wrong to drink a glass of liquor. Yet the statute proceeds as if it were a crime to drink, and the seller was a participator.

The sale of lottery tickets is forbidden; but it is because they are used in gambling, and gambling is against the law.

Bad houses are forbidden; it is because fornication is a crime under the law.

The sale of bad books is forbidden; but it is because they are bad in essence, and no one but a few criminals claims otherwise.

The sale of gunpowder and other regulative measures stand on different ground.

7   J

The action of prohibition is indirect ; it lays a penalty on a deed which is not a crime, which, in fact, never becomes a crime, but in certain contingencies leads a man into drunkenness, and thence he falls into crime. A process so winding and circuitous necessarily carries crooked ways and shaky proceedings[1] into the administration of the law itself. Prosecutors, advocates, and witnesses are all moving in a false light, which deranges the perspective of common justice and common judicial proceedings. The statute which forbids sale has been broken. The per-

---

[1] One Sypher, a longshoreman, was prosecuted by a liquor-dealer for perjury in a liquor case, and we cite from the report of the "Providence Journal," December 23 : — Sypher testified : " A bargain has been made between myself and Mr. Read (*i.e.*, the state constable) to furnish testimony in liquor cases." The state constable testified : " The defendant had entered into connection with the state constabulary, and made an agreement to furnish evidence in liquor cases." He made memorandums in a book furnished by the constable. Another witness testified that Sypher "stated that he had entered into a compact with the state constables, by which he was to receive $5 for every case in which he testified ; he was asked if he got $5 in case the prosecution failed, and my impression is that he answered that it made no difference whether the case failed or not." These are the artificial crimes which artificial laws breed and nourish.

son who participated in the act, the drinker, feels no sense of crime ; indeed, the law nowhere makes him criminal. The community in which the drinker moves — and a man rarely rises above the moral sense of those around him — do not regard the act of drinking as a crime. Then the penalty is out of all proportion to the offence involved. This affects the testimony, affects the prosecutor, affects the court. It is well known that it is hard to get a verdict for murder from a jury, every member of which carries a pistol in his pocket. The state is placed in a position where it creates crime out of a simple act, not in itself evil, pursues by testimony not fair in the ordinary sense, and convicts under an unwilling as well as blind justice. The whole process, from the inception of the law to the conviction of the criminal, is artificial and not vital.

This and almost every argument against prohibition is met by the rejoinder, " Society has a right to protect itself." When used in a general sense, this is one of those singular maxims or saws which Bentham terms a fancy. " What is this reason ? If it is not a distinct view of good or evil, it is a mere fancy; it is a despotism, which announces nothing but the interior persuasion of him who speaks."[1] Fully expressed, the saying would be, " Society is all-powerful. I think this act (whatever the same may be) is a proper exercise of its power. Others ought to think so. Therefore this act is right."

We think this widely diffused notion merely confounds the terms " sovereignty " and " right." The sovereign power is absolute and " is legally uncontrolled both from within and without." A large number of persons and a few commonwealths in the United States misinterpreted this plain truth about the year 1861, and great tribulation resulted thereby. An old fisherman, whom the writer knew, though a man of strong character, sometimes over-indulged in his cups. One cold night, when in this state he turned every member of his family out of doors, saying,

[1] Theory of Legislation, p. 74.

"I will be d—d if I don't show you Captain Barber lives here." This absolute principle is inherent in government; it is oriental. But it has been the business of civilized people of the Teutonic and Anglo-Saxon races especially to frame heavy checks and restraints which they have imposed on this authority; until the meanest citizen or smallest infant has rights before which supreme arbitrary power itself must fold its hands in dumb silence. " When the sovereign power commands its subjects to do or forbear from certain acts, the claim for such performances or forbearances which one person thereby has upon another, is called a *right;* the liability to such performances or forbearances is called a *duty;* and the omission of an act commanded to be done, or the doing of an act commanded to be forborne, is called a *wrong.*" [1]

" All sovereign legislatures, whether of one or many, are, and are alone, the sources from which all rights flow. Yet we hear of original rights, natural rights, &c. . . . All that

[1] Geo. Cornewall Lewis. Political Terms, p. 7.

those persons mean is, that in their opinion the claims which they call *rights* ought, in sound policy, to be sanctioned by law. It is the duty of such persons to show that sound policy requires what *they* require."[1]

The burden of proof lies on the maker of a statute. He must show that the proposed measure forbids something evil in itself. This makes a positive law against crime, which society knows to be crime. These statutes need no argument for their right to be; the question is merely one of methods. Or, in the second place, he must show that his measure is proper, in that it will prevent practices by which evil is directly incurred. The question then becomes one of experience; the statute-maker must above all things show that it will succeed.[2]

[1] Geo. Cornewall Lewis. Political Terms, pp. 23, 24.

[2] People talk of the easy success of these liquor statutes if this or that could be granted. They forget the inherent difficulties of the situation. We would say a States prison could keep its inmates from drinking. Yet in Sing Sing an astute convict entrusted with the vegetables managed to secrete potatoes, distilled them, and sold the whiskey to his fellows.

" The legislator is not the master of the disposi-
tions of the human heart, he is only their interpre-
ter and their minister. The goodness of the laws
depend upon their conformity to general *expectation.* . . . To become the controller of expectation,
the law ought to present itself to the mind as *certain to be executed;* at least no reason for presuming
the contrary ought to appear. Is there ground for
supposing that the law will not be executed? An
expectation is formed contrary to the law itself.
The law then, is useless. It never exercises its
power except to punish; and these inefficacious
punishments are an additional reproach to the law." [1]

It is not enough to show that there is great
evil at work, and to stop it would be a good
thing. The makers of these secondary statutes
must show by overwhelming testimony that
their principle of legislation will do the work
and accomplish its ends, or else there is no
foundation, no right of being, for the law itself.
All the rights of society, inherent or acquired,
cannot go beyond these two principles stated
above. A people drunk with a passion, whether
of anger or of fanaticism, may impose any stat-

[1] Bentham. Theory of Legislation, pp. 148, 153.

ute they please ; it may obtain an abstract foundation, just as our friend, Captain Barber, established his authority.   But although, in one sense, the sovereign power is never wrong, the great principles of justice finally upset the statute.   Nemesis pursues peoples and statutes as well as individuals.

For example, the use of fine bolted wheaten flour is a partial evil.   If a majority, however constructed, could impose a statute that every one should eat coarse hulled flour, this measure would fall within these fancied "rights," and establish itself as a function of the state.   It would none the less be a tyranny, and even after vested rights had been satisfied the law would never become a living success.   Fine white bread would taste sweeter than ever, and each man would say that he would decide for himself what flour his stomach should digest.

The liquor traffic, like other trades, has always been more or less controlled by statute law.   But the principle of prohibition is a new contrivance quite recently introduced.   It does

not undertake the control of a traffic, it under-
takes the control of the appetite of every individual so far as the beverage of alcoholic liquors
is concerned. We have shown that the statutes laid in this principle, so far from having
an " expectation " of success, have uniformly
failed. In application, they have never succeeded long enough to be called working
laws.

An odd conceit, we can hardly call it an argument, which the prohibitionists put forth, is the
claim that if you impose any restriction on the
seller of liquor, through requirement of license
or otherwise, you thereby take away the natural
right of the citizen to purchase, and thus establish the same principle as they attain through
prohibition. When the history of this legislation comes to be read in a disinterested time,
we venture to predict nothing will seem more
strange than this notion which is put forward
through one and another argument. According to this theory, the government has forbidden
and attempted to cut off about every action

7*

which enters into the daily life of the citizen. Look at a few instances.

The city provides that we shall give our refuse matter to licensed swill-carts. Does it thereby forbid the carrying away of garbage from our premises?

It licenses a few persons to sell gunpowder. Does it prevent every one from obtaining powder when he desires it?

It prevents the sale of adulterated milk, and obliges the milk-dealer to use a standard measure. Do these methods prevent us from getting milk when we desire it?

It allows no one but an authorized physician and pharmaceutist to prescribe and prepare medicines. Does that prevent us from obtaining arsenic to kill rats, although some people may use the poison for suicide?

They argue, in turn, that there is no parallel between regulation of milk, gunpowder, and similar traffic, and the sale of liquors, which is exceptional. This begs the question. The state would cut off the sale of liquor as a beverage, either because it is a poison always injurious, or because from actual experience it has found the prohibition useful. Now the poison theory of alcoholic liquors is at best in abeyance. It never was an established proof on which governmental interference could be based. Latterly science tends more and more in the opposite direction. As Dr. Hammond says, " If alcohol is not food, what is it? We have seen that it takes the place of food, and the weight of the body increases under its use." [1] On the other hand, we have shown that prohibition, instead of being a tried success, is a failure. The notion that there is no practical difference between a certain amount of prohibition and a certain amount of license is absurd logically and in fact. Certain principles of government are radically different. The mildest form of confiscation differs absolutely from the worst kind of taxation ever invented. So prohibition cuts off, while license permits. Those who

[1] Psychological and Medico-Legal Journal. July, 1874, page 10.

would make the former into the latter, are like the historical old woman who granted free permission that her boy should learn to swim. " Learn to swim by all means, but never go near the water."

We claim that in reviewing prohibition, both from our own point of view and from that of its advocates, we have proven that it is not a regulation of the liquor traffic. Regulation presupposes a use of liquors for a beverage, just as the common statutes look forward to a use of medicines or salt. The use of liquors as a beverage is a common and well-known fact. Prohibition proposes to interdict this use by a wholesale edict. It is not like forbidding the sale of poison to one intending suicide; this is an exceptional stoppage of a dark crime. The use of liquors as a beverage, whether they be food or not, is something which the majority of the community have adopted into their every-day life. With that common use of alcohol there goes an abuse which engenders among us a vast amount of vice and crime. To attempt to stop the abuse and evil consequences by forbidding the use, is no more practicable than it would have been to cut off the use of pork by statute because much pork held " trichinæ," and thus injured people. To prohibit the use of liquors by statute law — *i.e.*, to forbid their sale, which cuts off the legal enjoyment of them from all except the rich and strong — is not possible, and is wrong ; it is impossible, because it is wrong.

ANOTHER SYSTEM.

A LTHOUGH it is out of the direct line of
our argument, it accords with our moral
purpose to offer a substitute for the prohibitory
liquor laws. In our view, any system which
could be fairly executed would be better than
prohibition, which from its essential nature is
incapable of execution. The first condition of
any judicious system would be some substantial
accord among the main body of the people legislated for. 'Nearly all our legislation on this
subject has been initiated either by a small section of passionate reformers on the one hand, or
a section of liquor-dealers on the other. These
elements must ever be potent, but neither should
be, or need be, all-powerful. The whole community holds the main interest in this important question, and sooner or later this great

public, central good will assert itself and control
the wings of abstinence and free license according to its own larger and mastering judgment.
Great reforms always work out in this way.
The American nation thought for generations,
and honestly too, that slavery was a side issue,
affecting only fire-eaters or abolitionists. Sud-
denly it awakened to the consciousness that its
own life was in danger; then it settled the question, and settled it for the public good, not as
either party desired or would have believed
possible.

No principle can ever unite this great public sentiment, and weld it into effective action,
which is not founded on absolute justice. As
the matter stands before the law, a man desir-
ing a gill of whiskey or of beer has a right to it.
The contingent fact that he may add other gills
to his want, and thus make himself a drunkard
or a pauper, is in practical life too remote for the
law to control by forbidding the first want.
No legislation looking so far into future risks
ever did succeed. If a great mass of citizens

are moved by this desire, which cannot be shown to transgress a law of God, then it is the business of government to provide for the desire. The desire for the first glass of liquor is legitimate, and cannot be cut off by the risk or possibility of a fourth glass. A man who buys too much tenderloin steak may make himself dyspeptic, or the woman who buys a silk dress may make herself a pauper; but the law cannot look to such issues. This principle of individual liberty goes to the very foundations of every law, social custom, or personal opinion. It is too large and too important to be much affected by the evils of intemperance, great as those evils are, individually and socially. John Stuart Mill says: —

" Neither one person nor any number of persons is warranted in saying to another human creature of ripe years, that he shall not do with his life for his own benefit what he chooses to do with it. He is the person most interested in his own well-being ... the interest which society has in him individually (except as to his conduct to others) is fractional, and altogether indirect; while, with respect to his own feelings and circumstances, the most ordinary man or woman has means of knowledge immeasurably surpassing those that can be possessed by any one else." [1]

A few theorists place the basis of rights in society and not in the individual, holding that personal rights are privileges which society grants for its own good. The legitimate functions of society have been coherently developed to their fullest extent by Mr. Mulford, in his work on " The Nation." He gives the nation or society the powers and responsibilities of a moral being. But he definitely puts by the theory that society gives rights to the individual. " There is in the nation the institution, not the creation of rights, since their foundation is in the nature of man, and their affirmation is in the nation." [2]

It is established that the individual has in himself certain rights. When society transgresses these, it passes beyond the province of

---

[1] Mill on Liberty, p. 147.
[2] Mulford's Nation, p. 106.

law. As Professor Amos says, in another connection, it attempts to "deluge law with morals." Among these rights is that of drinking, so long as the drinker does not make himself a nuisance to others. However we may hedge him about, and restrain him, and prescribe the manner of his drinking and purchasing, for the social good, yet the original right cannot be extinguished, but remains unaffected. If my neighbor has a right of way across my estate, way must always be made for him. He cannot drive through my strawberry beds and clover fields; I can regulate that; but a good and sufficient way must always be kept open. When society deliberately cuts off the power of the citizen to purchase liquors in reasonable amounts, it commits an act of injustice, no matter how good the intention may be. That injustice cries out until it rights itself; it moves the foundations of society until the stone which the builders rejected becomes the head of the corner.

Therefore we say society, as a whole, must take up this matter, and base the regulation of

the traffic on the principles of justice and the
common sense of experience. We are met at
once by the rejoinder from prohibitionists, that
license laws have always failed in practice to
satisfy the community. Suppose they have
failed, that does not make prohibition just.
Latterly, the license laws, and especially in the
New England States, have been mere make-
shifts, the lax reactions which always follow
overstrained laws; they have been the immoral
result of over-moralization. The liquor dealers
have controlled them, and they have been administered in no thorough spirit of regulation.
The reason the liquor dealers have such strength
is because prohibitory attempts put such a force
of customers behind them. Take away this
unnatural pressure, give reasonable play to the
appetite of the individual, and then get his influence in restraining the traffic for the good
of society. The power of liquor dealers will
then shrink to its natural proportions like that
of other traders.

We can offer a system of regulated traffic

which is based on justice, respects the individual,
and is worked in every detail for the benefit of
the whole community, so far as this appetite
can be controlled by any mechanism. It has
the further advantage of success after more than
eight years of trial.

Sweden has always used liquors freely, and
abused them as well.' The people are northern
in race as we are, and their climate has always
favored a large consumption of spirits. One
town, after trying free license, then partial
licenses unsuccessfully, hit on the plan of con-
centrating all the licenses into one association which should represent the public. The
gradual growth of this system is detailed in
" Macmillan's Magazine " for February, 1872,
and October, 1873. We cite : —

"In [1] Gothenburg (the second town of Sweden,
a seaport with a manufacturing and trading population of 58,000 in 1872), all the public-house licenses
are held by a single ' retailing company,' incorporated
by royal charter. Each license representing, as with
us, the right to open one public-house, the directors

[1] " Macmillan," vol. 28, p. 522.

use in different parts of the town just so many of their licenses as they deem required by the population. In the first place, they take care that all houses in which liquor is sold are light, well ventilated, and roomy. Into each they put a manager, on the terms that he is to take all his supplies of spirits from the company, and to pay over to them every farthing received for spirits sold, his remuneration consisting of the profits on his sales of tea and coffee, malt liquors,[1] cigars, and eatables, supplemented, in most cases, by a fixed salary. Once a year the company's balance-sheet is submitted to and audited by the municipal authorities, and thereupon the entire amount of the net profits for the past twelve months is paid into the municipal treasury, and becomes part of the general revenue of the town. All this is an embodiment and earnest striving after the realization of sundry definite conclusions about the drink traffic at which the Gothenburgers arrived eight years ago. They embodied the results of their experience in the following four principles:[2] I. Spirits to be retailed without any profit whatever to the retailer, who can thus have no temptation to stimulate their consumption. II. The

---

[1] In "Sweden, a country of *spirit* drinkers, the trade in malt liquors has only quite recently been deemed important enough to require legislative regulation and restriction."

[2] "Macmillan," February, 1872, p. 311.

sale of spirits on credit, or on the security of pledges, to be stringently prohibited.   III. All houses in which the liquor trade is carried on to be well lighted, roomy, airy, and clean.   IV. Good victuals at moderate prices, to be always procurable in drinking-houses by anybody demanding them.   It was not in the nature of things that any private individual, trader or non-trader, should be found ready to carry out such a programme as this.   It was tolerably obvious that if the scheme was to be put through at all, a number of the leading members of the community mnst loosen their purse-strings and put their shoulders to the wheel together.   And this, thanks to the public spirit that has for years prevailed at Gothenburg, was done promptly and effectually.   Upon the requisition of an influential list of the townsmen, headed by several of the leading mercantile firms, the government granted a charter of incorporation to a company formed with the express object of working out a thorough reform of the local liquor trade, in accordance with the above principles.   By the terms of this charter the maximum nominal capital of the company is fixed at 200,000 rix-dollars, or rather more than £11,000.   Each shareholder is declared strictly liable up to the amount of his guarantee (*i.e.*, stock.)   It has not, however, been found necessary, so far, to call upon the shareholders for any part of their subscriptions.   Spirits may not be served to a person apparently intoxicated ('overloaded' is the expressive term in the act), nor to a minor; and the act, in its tender solicitude for the helpless tippler, provides that a person 'overloaded' is not to be turned out of the house. The Gothenburgers made up their minds that, though they could not stamp out the spirit trade, they could and must regulate it; and that their way of doing so should be to limit the number of spirit shops, to insure the purity of the spirits offered for sale, and, the most important point of all, to make it nobody's interest to stimulate the consumption, and by keeping these principles steadily in view, the Gothenburg company have been, and it may be hoped will continue to be, the means of diminishing substantially and permanently the sum-total of drunkenness and crime among their fellow-townsmen."

We do not like statistics in these matters, but the curious can trace out these figures:[1] —

"The percentages by police records of cases of drunkenness amongst the population have been: In 1864, 6.10; in 1865 (the company established at

[1] The "Fortnightly Review" says: "In Gothenburg the number of cases of *delirium tremens* has been diminished by one-third."

the beginning of October), 5.57; in 1866, 3.75; in
1867, 3.58; in 1868, 3.50; in 1869, 2.56; in 1370,
2.52; in 1871, 2.67; in 1872, 2.72."[1]

With the rise of wages came an increase
of drunkenness, but there was a deeper cause
of trouble: —

"Not the public-houses, but the 'retail' shops
are the offenders, — places where the holders of what
we term grocer-licenses sell spirits in quantities of a
half-*kan* (about a quart) and upwards, for consumption off the premises. This branch of the trade the
company has never hitherto been able to control.
There have been stumbling-blocks in the way of
their supplanting the private grocer-business; and
there still exists in the town no less than five and
thirty private shops of this class, constant thorns in
the company's side, conducted, as they naturally
are, with a view above all things to profit; and so
sedulously counteracting the endeavors of the company to discourage the consumption of alcohol. The
directors of the company know that cheap drink
spells drunkenness, and that high prices, in this as
in other trades, check consumption. So where they
are absolute masters of the situation, in the public
houses, they deliberately put a high price on the
spirits served; their tariff-price for a glass of *brän-*

1 Fortnightly Review, vol. 28, p. 522, *et seq.*

vin (corn-whiskey, the staple alcoholic drink of the country, and particularly of the lower classes) being 6 *öre*, which is at the rate of 3 rix-dollars per *kan*[1] (equivalent to 5s. 10d. per gallon); whereas they have to pay the distiller only 2s. 5d. per gallon. Now the 'retailers' or licensees may not sell less than a half-*kan* = about 25 ordinary dram-glasses, at a time. . . . So he gets a few kindred souls to practice 'salning' with him, that is, to club their small coins to make up the price of a half-*kan* at the spirit-grocers, carrying the liquor to the nearest convenient corner (for consumption on the premises would be directly illegal), and there drinking it."

They could not-reduce the amount of drunkenness further while this evil was at work: —

"We have done our best (says the company's report), but all our efforts are crippled while 'salning' continues, and 'salning' will continue so long as the grocer-licenses remain in private hands, and are worked with a view to private profit. We are convinced there is one remedy, and only one, for the present evil, and that is for the municipality to undertake the sole and entire management of the local *retail* spirit trade, on the same terms as we already work the public houses. . . . Last February a remarkable series of meetings was held

---

[1] "A *kan* is rather less than three-fifths of a gallon."

8

in Gothenburg. The Workingmen's Union sponta-
neously took this matter into consideration . . .
adopted two clear suggestive resolutions, which
were forwarded to the representatives of Gothenburg in the Diet, recommending (1) that the company should be entrusted with all spirit-licenses,
grocer as well as public-house; and (2) an increased
excise duty on spirits, with the sure concomitant of
higher retail prices. The new law will come into
operation October, 1874." [1]

In another year we shall learn how this new
feature works in practice : —

"What the company will do with their monopoly, may be pretty well predicted from their
past conduct. They will keep open only so many
'grocer' spirit shops as may be competent to supply the natural unstimulated demand of the population. They will deliberately handicap these shops
by so raising their prices, that for the quart of 25
drams of bränvin there will be charged something
like the price of 25 separate drams at the public-
house, thus removing the fundamental reason and
attraction of the 'salning' trick."

[1] "Since above was written the auction has taken place.
After a keen competition *twenty-five* licenses were disposed
of, for (in the aggregate) £2,000 more than *thirty-five* fetched
last year, — a fact which shows the large profits realized
lately by the private licenses. (August 14)."

Scotland, naturally first influenced by Sweden, and a country which struggles hard with drunkenness, is moving rapidly toward this system. " The General Assemblies (in May) of the three principal church bodies of Scotland, the Presbyterian Synod, the Established, and the Free Church, have dwelt upon it with marked emphasis and approval." The " London Spectator,"[1] in commenting on the system, says : —

"The merits of this system are conspicuous. They will be generally recognized, and the recognition cannot fail largely to affect the final judgment of the public as to its feasibility. Of course its grand recommendation is that it utterly disowns the prohibitive crotchet of your fanatical 'Permissionists.' It refuses to treat the question as if it were capable of being solved in the simple and direct manner that might apply to the choice of Hercules. It takes another ground from that of regarding it as a question between virtue and vice, virtue being typified in the austere respectability of the permissive prohibitionist, and vice in the portly form of the publican. So far we deem it rational and well-considered."

[1] " Spectator," October 18, 1873.

A few figures will show what the payments
to the town revenue from this source have
been. "In 1865, the company held thirty-nine
licenses and paid in 50,782 rix dollars. Gradually increasing in 1871, the company held
all = 61 licenses, and paid in 191,759 rix dollars," or, in round numbers, 97,000 United
States gold dollars.

The direct gains in money to the community through this system are great; the indirect are still greater, and cannot be measured.
To begin with some of the more remote, the
testimony of Gothenburgers shows an immense
gain in the lessening of the traffic, and thereby
a lessening of money expended for the indulgence, and consequently a lessening of poverty
and crime. The taking away of the profits
from the common liquor-dealers is a collateral
advantage hardly to be estimated, for these
profits are too often badly used. The gain to
the revenue is large, and is something which
every tax-payer can see with the keen vision
which affects the pocket more than the optical

nerve. Any man or woman who sees a hundred
thousand dollars or a proportional sum going
into the treasury of his town, will be a good
special constable, though he may not hold a
partisan appointment from the state, to help
enforce the law against illicit traffic in liquors.
The opposition of the lower end of the liquor
trade would be strong, but it would lose that
tremendous representative weight which its
backing of customers now gives it in every
political agitation. Decent men, and not the
indecent, make the strength of the liquor dealer's custom, and they would rally to the support of this system, for each one would see that
his own material as well as moral interest was
furthered by paying the profits of his own
drinking into the town coffers instead of the till
of the common dealer. The importance of this
detail will not so much weigh with some good
women, or those earnest, impatient men who can
see no good in enlisting the common, selfish
motives of mankind in the service of the right.
Men skilled in legislation and administration,

however, know at once that no law works so easily or so well as that which secures the co-operation of a great mass of citizens through the details of its own operation.

All these issues of the system are subordinate to the main question; is it true, is it right? The extreme prohibitionist will answer, with a shriek, that no sale of liquor for a beverage can be right. We have argued to little purpose, if we have not proved that this opinion is not held by any large number of persons, and, from the nature of the case, cannot be sustained by any large number so long as men are as they are. The conscientious abstinent would be released from his unsatisfactory tugging at an impossible law, and enabled to turn his efforts toward a change in the inclinations of the drinker. We should have incorporated in this system all that the law can accomplish. First, a privilege is secured to every individual of supplying any want of his appetite which under the law is legitimate; secondly, all the fruits of this privilege are husbanded for the use and benefit of society. Society incurs a certain risk whenever an individual drinks, — a risk which is beyond that of the individual. As some compensation for this risk, it receives all the commercial profit, and retains control of the operation under the wisest rules it can enjoin. Turn the question whichever way we may, this is the uttermost the state can accomplish; no ideal government could get more out of the law than these two principles yield. The absolute interdiction of the natural appetite is beyond the power of any government, and must be reached by other means than statute law. The individual on his own ground is mighty against the pressure of the state, or of society in mass; but he is weak and helpless against the moral assaults of other individuals. No one can withhold his ear from the appeal of an earnest moralist. There is the ground where the abstinent can reach the appetite of the individual, and there only.

This system would require some change, but not much, to adapt it to our American life. First, we must have a strong public sentiment in its favor; then the wise men, the strong men of affairs, the administrative men in any community, must take hold, and carry the principle into successful operation. Whether it could succeed in cities like New York and London would be matter of experiment; but there is every reason for its success in cities of moderate size or towns. We would open one restaurant with such a license for every one thousand inhabitants in a town, and grant a grocer's or package license for every three thousand or four thousand people. This would give about one place for sale or drinking in large towns and villages where there are now five to ten. In sparse districts the diminution would be less. If the practice of "salning" or clubbing drinks should obtain, then we would follow the Swedish example, and concentrate all the licenses in the one company of each town. Probably this practice would not be relatively so potent in America, yet it might interfere with the best working of the system. Still it would be better to come to the result gradually, through the convictions of the people, and not to start with all the pressure of a close monopoly. We should likewise be careful, over-careful even, in limiting the consumption by exorbitant prices. The American people, though wonderfully patient, as these absurd prohibitory statutes well show, yet do not like to be governed too much. The higher prices should be made the greater the inducements to illicit traffic; and, in our view, illicit traffic aggravates the evils of drinking enormously. We would have no secret places for drinking. If it is a good thing for a young man "to take a drink," then it is good to take it openly. If he needs it, he should not be ashamed of the fact, and the whole public sentiment would soon come to an expression of these principles. The sort of half-sympathy which now goes with the dodging of an impossible law would be taken away from a fellow who skulked in holes, when every reasonable want should be gratified. This would not absolutely keep young men from error, but, in another method, though by the same principle as we indicated in the legal method, it would do for them all that a wholesome public opinion could do.

Public sentiment can assist the individual, and draw him by a wise sympathy toward a better development of himself. It cannot make him, nor refashion him by statute law or wholesale clamor into a being differing from his own nature.

IMMORAL LAW-MAKING.

———◆———

"GENTLEMEN," said Edmund Burke, " bad laws are the worst sort of tyranny. In such a country as this they are of all bad things the worst. Worse by far than anywhere else; and they derive a particular malignity even from the wisdom and soundness of the rest of our institutions."[1]

Human law is a mighty force; it faintly reflects the ordering power of Omnipotence itself. On the infinite side it is little and full of error; on the finite side, in our actual life, it is majestic, and is the grandest reality we know. It is so great a blessing that generally we are not conscious of it, as we breathe and see unconsciously, though light and air are the greatest of natural facts. The parts of law and lawful order which we do see are the least parts, and those which

[1] Rivington's Ed., III. 426.

give to the vulgar mind its notions of the province and character of legal administration.
Punishing criminals and adjusting the selfish
conflict of rights is not the main province of
law, though here it commonly manifests itself,
and many do not look beyond these superficial
results.   The true action of law, that which
makes or unmakes society, just as breathing
affects the body for good or ill, lies deeper
down, and embodies our living; — embodies it
on the human and earthward side, as religion or
the spirit of God with us embodies it on the‘
heavenward side.   After all, what does the
illuminated righteousness of a man do for his
neighbors, unless he embodies it in " positive
morality," as Mr. Austin terms it, or the moral
order of the law, — something which enters into
the actual living of the citizen, which is tangi-
ble, and goes to the making of a state, just as
plank and timber go into the hull of a ship?

The common idea of innocence and natural
simplicity is pictured in the free life of the
farmer at the plough, tilling his field in joyous

hope, and free from the cares which social restraint and artificial laws have netted around less favored creatures. When did this natural farmer ever exist since the gates of Paradise closed on an idle recipient of God's bounty, and opened the world to a laboring partner of the Creator himself? What savage ever tilled his field without the harsh control of his chief, or a bitter struggle with his enemy? Wretched as the interior of Africa is, yet Schweinfurth found order and government, despotic but effective. "One of the most influential personages of the neighboring race of the Lao was a woman already advanced in years, of the name of Shol. She played an important part as a sort of chief in the Meshera, her riches, according to the old patriarchal fashion, consisting of cattle." The New England Puritan, with gun and axe on either side of his plough, subduing the wild wood while he watched for the wilder savage, symbolizes the whole struggle which civilized man has carried on with nature and the natural man.

Instituted law has come out of this long struggle ; not the mere policeman's club, though his
badge carries the whole history upon it, but the
pure spirit of order diffused through society,
moving according to law, and not under the
restraints of the law. It is not religion nor
family life themselves, but it is to them as the
bones are to the body, or the body is to the
soul.

It is an error, more or less common, that liberty lies outside instituted law or social order.
That individual freedom is a something which
man has kept back, while surrendering little by
little of his natural rights in the developing
contests, we have indicated above. In fact,
there never was any such freedom or liberty
since Adam began to board himself, instead of
being fed as a brute is fed. He then had to
consult Eve, and she was obliged to consult him,
or they would have had a sorry dinner. Thus
the family developed, and the state came afterward. An individual is little more than a
mathematical point or line without breadth or

thickness. In combination with others he finds his own powers, and builds the man, as we understand him, out of his intercourse with other men. The liberty a savage values was not the right to catch a fish or dig a yam, but the power to keep them, and to find his wife and children in his hut after he returned from a search after other rights ; and he at once surrendered whatever he had to his chief, that he might have the liberty which comes through order, and cannot exist individually or unlimited by other liberties. It is through society and through law that we enjoy those individual rights which are so finely adjusted we cannot see the restraints, and call them natural, just as we call a beefsteak natural, though it is the result of long ages of fostering care applied by man to nature. This principle was laid down by Aristotle, and has been well developed by many great writers : —

"There is, indeed, no doubt that a wandering savage, who has occupied a plot of ground, possesses the power of using his limbs, and cultivating his land; but to suppose that these liberties are, under a settled government, only spared by the legislature, and not created and secured by it, betrays a complete misapprehension of legal rights, and the acts of a sovereign body. Under an established government, no absence of law can be beneficial; because every act which may be done by man must be either permitted or prohibited by the legislature. What the law does not forbid it sanctions; and will protect those who do it from obstruction." [1]

We have purposely taken the broadest possible theory of social rights, that we might show Burke's meaning when he says that a bad law in a good government is the worst tyranny. It is because law has so wound itself in with every strand of civilization, that any wrong produced by it becomes doubly severe. Some things could be done under rude civilizations by law, *i.e.*, by statute, which cannot be done successfully now. Under a theocratic rule it was easy to prevent people from eating pork; and that seemed to be a wise use of the governing force to the best legislators of that time. What

[1] George Cornewall Lewis, Use and Abuse of Political Terms, p. 200.

civilized man would think of prohibiting pork to-day? Yet government is stronger to-day than it was under a theocracy. It has grown stronger by relegating certain matters to the individual, living, as we have described above, in an atmosphere of law, so that he needs no statutes in those affairs. His food and drink, clothing and expenditure, are now left to him who is a law unto himself; yet all these matters were once an anxious concern to the legislator. Suppose our abstinence friends, or any other party, should enact a statute that no person should eat over eleven ounces of meat per diem. In itself, it would probably be a good regulation. It would do some harm, but would injure fewer people than it would benefit in this American world, if it were carried out by every individual. Such a statute would at once show the limits which civilization has imposed upon itself, for it could not be carried into effect. Voracious eaters would be hurt by the tyranny, and lesser ones, by dreading it, would feel the same sense of oppression. A father of a family

would not undertake this method of controlling
eating; and no state has ever possessed power
equal to the paternal for controlling individual
action, where the acts are numerous and frequent. Such matters in a higher civilization
have passed out of statute law into that higher
moral region which is a consequence and concomitant of law, but is the proper home of the
individual.

Theocratic legislators overlook this principle,
or are ignorant of it. We say, Burke would
say, a law ill-advised and badly executed is
worse than the crime or injuries it would restrain. They say, " No. God's laws stand in
statute, though they are constantly broken; it
is our duty to maintain the liquor statute, broken or not." [1]

The difference is readily comprehended by any
one not blinded by his prejudices. Human laws
are penal, and the offender escapes the penalty
if the statute is badly adjusted. God's laws
are vital, and carry their penalty not in a punish-

[1] Those arguments are actually used in Rhode Island.

ment, but in a consequence, which no human being ever escaped in this world, whatever the world to come may yield. For these and other obvious reasons wise legislators have abandoned more and more of the theocratic grounds of law and based their legislation on right reason and experience. The present agitation to legislate God into the Constitution of the United States is an example. Common sense at once met this effort with the fact: He is there through the great fundamental ideas which are in our people; if not there by means of these, you cannot put Him there by statute law.

In running counter to these great truths, — bloody axioms the world has fought out, sweet axioms it has unfolded in the ways of peace, — our fanatical friends do a wrong they know not of. We have shown these liquor statutes to be badly grounded in law, — a tyranny possible only through the irresponsibility of the voting majority ; to be badly executed, actually defied, and maintained because they are so easily defied or evaded. Dr. Miner says : " If the Angel

Gabriel should come down to earth and sell
liquors as beverages, he would not lift the business up to heaven, but the business would drag
the angel down to hell." [1] The reason of this
is plain, and is found in the principle Burke
states. The better the social system, the worse
will be the effect of a bad law. A home may
be briefly turned into a hell by a few bad principles.

It is no figure of speech that when you make
an impossible law and maintain it by fraud and
tyranny, you make a hell on earth, and change
an angel into a demon. We say fraud deliberately, for up to this point we have treated the
prohibitionists as a whole, and with the respect
their main motive entitles them to. But bad
laws do not stop with the main motive; they
drag other influences in their train. One of
the worst consequences of this legislation is the
wretched puling hypocrisy which it directly
creates and encourages. In our first chapter
we described the process by which politicians

[1] Miner's Argument, p. 110.

are evolved out of the abstinence pressure when it is passing from the moral into the political sphere. We only dwelt on the necessary results of such laws in that view. There is another view which people who uphold these statutes must see sooner or later. There is a strong appetite for liquors diffused in society, not the drunkard's appetite, but that more potent, because unseen, power which compels many respectable men to use liquors. Whether it be wise or unwise, good or bad, that appetite remains, and will not be abolished by a statute law. It prevails more among the classes which rule society and manage politics. Relatively we mean, and not in disparagement of those classes. Men of strong natures, natural leaders in small communities, abounding in animal spirits, are more likely to drink than the average citizen, the average conference leader, or Sunday-school teacher. These men govern society so far as administration goes; they always will govern it in some way or other, — whether temperance, know-nothingism, or anti-slavery

prevails. These men, whether they be the
Joneses we have described, or the men who
make the legislators, the ward-meeting or cross-
road Warwicks, are driven into a hypocritical
obeisance to liquor legislation, which is false;
they are absolutely forced into a legal compli-
ance and a public phylactery broadening, even
if they do not conceal their personal habits,
as they sometimes do. Add to this element of
enforced pharisaism the nasty, foul, hybrid
creatures who feign a virtue when they have
it not, and drink secretly while in public they
maintain temperance, prohibition, total abstinence, and the semblance of any virtue their
snivelling natures can contain, and we have a
nice combination, not to say mixture, for the
administration of law or " positive morality."

Now, what sort of society is it into which
these influences reach? There are a few respectable and honorable dealers left in the
business of retailing spirits. The number of
such is small and daily growing less, while the
sum of sellers grows larger. The majority of

these dealers are foreign-born, and bred up in
the manner Dr. Miner describes, under the influences the prohibitionists have created. Their
field of operations is among aliens and Americans alike. The political education of many of
our citizens to-day, youthful Americans ˙and
the adult immigrants, is being carried forward
in a society which knows no law but force,
no wisdom but cunning. A man cannot buy
under the law to-day ˙in the city of Providence a spoonful of liquor to drink, nor a jug of
cooking wine. Yet it is notorious that men do buy
about what they please, if they desire to drink,
and are not of the very small class who regard a
prohibitory law as binding. Government, law,
social order itself, touch these heedless youth,
and these old children coming from abroad,
with no sufficient knowledge of the sublime
spirit of law described above; at this point
where their passions and appetites crop out in
their daily living. The political education of
these foreigners, and of such Americans as fall
under the same influences, is largely affected by

the same causes. To them there is no harmonious system of laws working toward better
morals in the community, but a struggle of force
with natural appetite. Their ears are closed to
reason, their consciences dulled to moral persuasion, because they only see force — tyrannical
force — bearing down a traffic which to them
seems legitimate, — which is legitimate on one
side of the law. As shown previously, the
state makes the liquors property, people all
around are actually drinking them, yet the
officers of the law are at work in spasmodic
efforts trying to destroy property which is con-
demned by the moral sentiment of a·party in
the state, while it has not lost its character and
its rights under the common law of the land.

What notions of property of social order and
of right must a man receive, who for years is
passing through such experience. If society
steadily adhered to the prohibition principle,
and faithfully worked it out, the result would
be bad enough. For the reasons given in an
early chapter, they have not been steady nor

faithful, and never will be. Like causes produce like effects. Until the habits of the people change, these laws must always be log-rolled through other political interests. They will be, as they have generally been, adroit political speculations, partially executed in spasms, then neglected when the temporary enthusiasm has cooled.

One of the latest English writers thus discourses on the crimes legislation creates within the state. If he had written with the experience of our liquor legislation before him, he could hardly have characterized it more exactly : —

"The creation of artificial crimes, and the consequent reckless onslaught on public liberty, form the most perilous temptations to which a modern statesman is exposed. The ignorance and the unhappy perverseness of the bulk of the population is still so considerable in modern states, that they present no barrier against the most enticing and hazardous political experiments, while they offer the most ready though treacherous arguments for the stern necessity of having recourse to those experiments.

The inevitable result is general paralysis of moral responsibility; executive tyranny in obscure places, and practised especially on classes of persons unable to attract public attention for their defence; a servile habit of reliance on government for the instant remedy of every evil, — including those which are the direct consequences of voluntary vice or self-indulgence; and the existence of a wide-spread network of police inspection and *espionage*, sapping the essential vital force of a free, self-reliant, and self-respecting national life." [1]

This corruption of legislation, this administering of moral purposes in such manner that they develop immoral results, is a modern innovation. It is one of the final issues of party politics.

Hear what De Tocqueville said about 1832: —

" Hitherto no one in the United States has dared to advance the maxim that every thing is permissible for the interests of society, — an impious adage, which seems to have been invented in an age of freedom to shelter all future tyrants. Thus, while the law permits the Americans to do what they please, religion prevents them from conceiving, and forbids them to commit what is rash or unjust."

---

[1] Sheldon Amos, Systematic View of Jurisprudence, p. 514.,

We have changed all that bravely. Now we have whole religious organizations pressing forward tyrannical laws, and devout apostles of finance, with politico-ecclesiastical machinery, forcing lobby-granted railway bonds on credulous people.

We do not mean to mix inconsequent topics, but we must consider whither we drift, and that all these symptoms show diseases; not necessarily one disease, but the different disorders are more or less related. Remember that the solvency of law is in the moral strength of the community, and at this moment we cannot afford to waste an atom of moral force in the maintenance of bad laws. The harm these worthy persons have done the State by pushing their good intentions beyond their legitimate sphere, is something which has not yet borne all its fruits, and which must be grappled with before it is too late. A great philosopher said men should possess a certain "indifferency" before they could pursue ethical truth with any advantage to themselves or their fellows. As we

understand moral science, a man, be he clergyman, lawyer, merchant, or day-laborer, will make
a poor decision in a matter pertaining to public
morals, unless his mind be open and free to receive all possible knowledge from without his
own special province. Few of us can grasp the
details of law, social science, or theology; but
any intelligent person can acquire the general
and leading principles which prevail in the
knowledge of his time. He is then, if candid
and earnest, in fit condition to hear and decide
an ethical question, which, as between man and
man, is the sum of knowledge or the province of
wisdom. Any one of us should pursue his own
personal interests, his likes and dislikes, his am-
bitions and pleasures, with the ardent force of
an honest advocate. This gives life and energy
to society as a whole, everybody is alive, as we
say. When these interests pass beyond himself
and affect others directly, as when he votes,
serves on a jury, administers an estate, acts
on a committee, although he is the same man,
other relations affect his moral state. The

legitimate passion of self sobers into the ethical opinion which reaches beyond himself and puts him into the attitude of a quick-eared but steady-minded judge, to carry out the figure with which we began.

Instead of that, a certain class of persons, frequent in every community, as Locke says, "begin with espousing the *well-endowed* opinions in fashion; and then seek arguments to show their beauty, or to varnish and disguise their deformity."

This is the precise attitude which the temperance party has held toward other moral questions for some thirty years. The writer has conversed with many sincere total abstinence men, who sadly admitted they had no hope in liquor laws, yet confessed that, whenever they differed with their associates, they were classed at once with free rum and the Sons of Belial. An end must come to this social despotism. Our quarrel with the prohibitionists goes far beyond the superficial statutes they enact. We arraign them at the bar of justice for the deceit and truckling cowardice they bring into social living, the disorder and confusion they drag into the ethics of law. We do not mean to overwhelm the reader with citations from Dr. Miner's argument; but he is a representative man, and the position and influence of ordinary and worthy prohibitionists can only be understood when their principles are worked out in full statement.

"How shall we explain the fact that so many godly men, conscientious men, are in this error? . . . I solemnly aver before you that, if any man — any young man especially — steps into a Boston pulpit and is silent for six months on this question of the character of the liquor traffic, he will find himself surrounded by a class of wealthy men, who will invite him to their homes, seduce him by the wine-cup, and lay him under obligation in a thousand ways. Whenever he finds himself degraded to this humiliating condition, though he may remain in the pulpit, he has ceased to be a minister of God." [1]

Who are these men, clergymen and others, he puts into the same category? The Rev. Doctors Adams, Leonard Bacon, Blagden,

[1] Miner's Argument, p. 76.

Hedge, Neale, Bishop Eastburn; Governors Andrew, Clifford, and Washburn; Agassiz; Doctors Bowditch, Charles T. Jackson, Holmes, H. J. Bigelow, Clarke; citizens Norcross, Lincoln, Duncan, and a hundred others. These men are among the topmost in their several vocations, and their professions cover nearly all the lines of our social life. They are the flower of New England, in so far as its blossoms can be gathered in one community. The pivots on which your living, good reader, and my living turns; the models to which we shall point our children, and ask them to imitate. For character far away affects us little; it is the men of our own time who impress themselves on us and on those coming next after. These men, and others like them, make our manners, in the higher sense, in which these are the fruit of the man, and not merely an external form or temporary custom. Legislate, cultivate, theorize as you will, it is in the best men and women of the day humanity finds itself, and seeks to know and improve itself. Is it good law, good morals, good religion, which reviles these illustrious citizens and holds them up for execration, because their opinion in a matter of diet and social habit or political action differs from another respectable party of voters and moralists? A petty spirit, narrowing daily, accelerating through our social mechanisms, impels the average unthinking moralist to enforce his social or political hobby on those unlike himself. Is this a process which will breed nobler and better men? Are we so rich in heroes that we need no more Andrews or Agassizs in this western world?

This great theme — the essential dignity and moral worth of human law — cannot be reached in a paragraph, nor dismissed in a volume. That view of it we have attempted to set forth — its partial relation with moral reform and humane impulse — is far-reaching and widely extended. No one person can grasp the whole topic; but we claim that we have established certain principles, both by the facts of experience and by those dictates of reason which control the nature of law, and ultimately control governmental action.

If the narrow theory of abstinence ever becomes the common basis of social life, the result must come through the agency of the individual acting on his fellows in ethical effort. Any civil pressure instituted to forward such result would not hasten but retard it. The individual must have his freedom, even to injure himself, and must not be restrained until his acts directly injure other persons. This gives the individual, while he has his senses, the right of drinking, and forbids the state from entirely cutting off the supply of liquors or from prohibition. In the second place, if temperance in drinking liquors continues to be, as it has been, the social habit of a large majority of the people, it must allow an equal freedom to the individual. The individual cannot be cut off from his normal activity because social good may in an uncertain contingency be harmed. His normal act must be wrong, or directly harmful in its effects, before the law can justly interfere and stop him. If society passes beyond this limit and oppresses the individual, it transcends its

9*

own laws of being, for it was created to develop the individual. When it loses this per-
ception and oppresses him, it finally loses its
vital force and extinguishes itself: for there
can be no society without individuals; an individual might exist without society, but a society,
without individuals would be impossible. This
principle is the foundation of justice, which, as
Madison says, is the end and aim of all societies,
No part of any structure is comparable to its
foundation; we can change any part; the
groundwork sustains the whole, and cannot
in itself be changed. All the benevolence of
an angel could not alter these principles. An
individual can save himself, his fellow can save
him, if the benevolent impulse is wisely di-.
rected. An individual is in some respects
greater than the state. But the nature of
justice cannot be altered by benevolence.
Justice can move all else, itself excepted. Dr.
Winship could lift nine hundred pounds; he
could not lift his own feet. The basis is im-
movable; humanity must rest somewhere in its

physical action, and God has given us no surer ground than justice; mercy may temper, it cannot change the nature of justice.

The cause of the failure of the prohibitory statutes is not in their parts; it is not because the quantity prohibited is too large or too small, the fines and imprisonment too lenient or too severe, the officers of state too slow or too quick, — it is in their whole, in the basis of the laws themselves. They are unjust. The law is a lie; whenever it attempts to execute itself, it lies and deceives. To say that worthy citizens have made up their minds they will have such laws, does not change their nature. The American people had made up their mind in immense majority that they would maintain slavery about the year 1852. Did that change the nature of justice? How long did slavery last?

Our prohibitory statute-makers, working on a benevolent motive, have debauched politicians, corrupted legislatures, and soiled the processes of courts, in the administration of these laws. This is disorder, and society should be in itself the highest order.   The broad and loyal Richard Hooker says : —

" Wherefore that we may briefly end ; of law there can be no less acknowledged than that her seat is the bosom of God, her voice the harmony of the world ; all things in heaven and earth do her homage, the very least as feeling her care, and the greatest as not exempted from her power ; both angels and men and creatures, of what condition soever, though each in different sort and manner, yet all with uniform consent, admiring her as the mother of their peace and joy."

Appetite is one of the lowest and meanest of divine creations ; yet what creature exists without it, what action can accomplish itself which goes not hand and hand with it ?   Life, the very emanation of divine being, is itself chained to it ; a royal master ever depending on this perpetual slave.   It is the intention and aim of man to live, but the motive impulse to that living is in the spring of the appetite.   Physical destruction of appetite is physical death.

In the moral world, the state can regulate and care for appetite ; it cannot kill that meanest creature of God. When the harmony of law is broken, when power attempts this ethical murder, the little creature outdoes mighty states, for it rests itself on that pure justice which is in the being of God!

APPENDIX.

———◆———

THERE is no complete and harmonious state-ment of the relation of alcohol to the animal economy to be found. The people have an old and common saying that "wine is the milk of old age." They do not say that it is cow's milk, nor that old age needs a poison to nourish it. On the other hand, the universal word "intoxicated" means poisoned; and it is almost certain that when a man is overdosed with liquor he is as if he were poisoned. These two conclusions of the common mind — first, that it is almost a food, and second, that it becomes in excess as dangerous as a poison — are very near to the scientific conclusions which we must draw from the excerpts which follow, and which are drawn from the most weighty authorities.

The following propositions represent fairly, as we believe, the present state of physiological knowledge on this subject : —

I. Alcohol is a substance which is used in the animal economy, and not wholly eliminated. The conditions of this use, or its exact mode of working in the body, are in doubt.

II. The question whether it acts as a positive food or a stimulant is in doubt. Late investigators lean more and more toward the food theory.

III. Most authorities agree that in moderate doses it diminishes bodily waste, like tea and coffee. Some, however (including among these advocates of the food theory), hold that tea and coffee do not diminish waste, and they put alcohol into the same class.

We are permitted to cite from studies made by Mr. Amasa M. Eaton : —

" In one sense, alcohol, that is, pure alcohol, is a poison ; but the confusion here consists in having two meanings in mind, and in passing unconsciously from one to the other, supposing both to be alike. Dr. Percy ('An Experimental Enquiry concerning the Presence of Alcohol in the Ventricles of the Brain,' &c., London, 1839) injected from two to four ounces of strong alcohol into the stomachs of dogs. Death followed, as well it might, the alcohol he used containing about eighty per cent of absolute alcohol. The strongest brandy and whiskey contain but fifty-four per cent of alcohol. The same quantity of solutions of this strength of tobacco, tea, coffee — perhaps even of salt — would produce the same result ; but as this is not the form or manner in which alcohol is ever administered, no reasoning can be drawn from such results. That pure alcohol (like many other substances, if taken pure, but which never are so taken) is a poison, is a statement there is no use in proving or adducing as evidence, for none will deny it.

"Lallemand, Perrin, and Duroy ('Du Role de l'Alcohol et des Anesthetiques dans l'Organisme,' Paris, 1860) are advocates of total elimination, in which view they are supported by many others, but not by the latest experimenters. To the same effect is Dr. Victor Subbotin, in the 'Zeitschrift für Biologie,' Heft IV. On the other hand, Dr. Anstie ('Stimulants and Narcotics,' and in various articles in the Medical Journals), after experiments made in consequence of Lallemand, Perrin, and Duroy's results, came to the conclusion that the original common opinion was right, and that only a small portion of any alcohol taken is eliminated unaltered. These results have been confirmed by Dupré ('On the Elimination of Alcohol,' read before the Royal Society, of which an abstract may be found in 'The Practitioner' for March, 1872).

"'First. The amount of alcohol eliminated per day does not increase with the continuance of the alcohol diet; therefore all the alcohol consumed daily must, of necessity, be disposed of daily; and as it certainly is not eliminated within that time, it must be destroyed in the system.

"'Second. The elimination of alcohol following the taking of a dose or doses of alcohol is completed twenty-four hours after the last dose of alcohol has been taken.

"'Third. The amount of alcohol eliminated in both breath and urine is a minute fraction only of the amount of alcohol taken.'

"Still more to the point are the experiments and

results of Dr. Hammond ('Effects of Alcohol on the Nervous System — Inaugural Address as President of the Neurological Society of New York,' published in 'The Psychological and Medico-Legal Journal' for July, 1874). He performed three series of experiments on himself, taking alcohol, first, when the food taken was just sufficient for the wants of the organism; second, when it was not sufficient; and third, when it was more than sufficient. Of course I have not space here to give any sufficient explanation of these and other experiments made, as quoted above. For all details I must refer the curious reader to the memoirs cited. Dr. Hammond says, in summing up: ' After such results, are we not justified in regarding alcohol as food? If it is not food, what is it? We have seen that it takes the place of food, and that the weight of the body increases under its use. Any substance which produces the effects which we have seen to attend on the use of alcohol is essentially food, even although it is not demonstrable at present that it undergoes conversion into tissue. If alcohol is not entitled to this rank, many substances which are now universally placed in the category of aliments must be degraded from their positions.'

. " ' Alcohol retards the destruction of the tissues. By this destruction force is generated, muscles contract, thoughts are developed, organs secrete and excrete. Food supplies the material for new tissue. Now, as alcohol stops the full tide of this decay, it is very evident that it must furnish the force which is developed under its use. How it does this is not clear. But it is not clear how a piece of iron deflects a magnetic needle when held on the opposite side of a stone wall or a feather bed. Both circumstances are ultimate facts, which, for the present at least, must satisfy us. That alcohol enters the blood and permeates all the tissues, is satisfactorily proven. Lallemand, Perrin, and Duroy contend that it is excreted from the system unaltered. If this were true of *all* the alcohol ingested, its action would be limited to its effects upon the nervous system, produced by actual contact with the nervous tissues; but there is no more reason to suppose that *all* the alcohol taken into the system is thus excreted unaltered from the body, than there is for supposing that all the carbon taken as food is excreted from the skin and lungs as carbonic acid. It is not at all improbable that alcohol itself furnishes the force directly, by entering into combination with the first products of tissue decay, whereby they are again assimilated, without being excreted as urea, uric acid, &c. Many of these bodies are highly nitrogenous, and under certain circumstances might yield their nitrogen to new tissues. Upon this hypothesis, and upon this alone, so far as I can perceive, can be reconciled the facts that an increase of force and a diminution of the products of the decay of tissue attend upon the ingestion of alcohol.' . . .

"'It would be only fair to ask me what constitutes excess? and if you did, I should answer that, in the abstract, I do not know, any more than I know how much tea or coffee any one of you can drink with comfort or advantage; how many cigars you can smoke without passing from good to bad effects; how much mustard on your beef agrees with you, or how much disagrees; or how much butter you can eat on your buckwheat cakes. In fact, I do not know that you can use any of these things without injury; for to some persons tea and coffee and tobacco and mustard and butter are poisonous. Every person must, to a great extent, be a law unto himself in the matter of his food; no one can *à priori* tell him what and how much are good for him. A single glass of wine may be excess for some individuals, while to others it fills a *rôle* which nothing else can fill. That alcohol even in large quantities is beneficial to some persons is a point in regard to which I have no doubt; but these persons are not in a normal condition, and when they are restored to health their potations should cease.'

"Dr. Curtis, of New York, says: 'In ordinary amounts alcohol is wholly consumed, transformed in the system, and, by the nature of its chemical composition, is capable, like certain elements of ordinary food, of thus yielding *force* which can be used by the economy to do life-work, &c. And thus, within certain limits of dose, alcohol is transformed like ordinary food in the system without producing any injurious effects, and, yielding useful force for the purposes of the economy, must be considered as a *food* in any philosophical sense of the word.' I wish to call particular attention to what he further says: 'It is an important point to know, and one little understood, that this food-action is attended with no exciting or intoxicating influence; but the whole effect, like that of ordinary food, is seen in the maintenance or restoration, according to circumstances, of that balance of function called health. But if taken in greater quantity than can be utilized as a force-yielding food, the excess of alcohol acts as a poison, producing a well-known train of perturbations of function. *All* signs of departure from the natural condition in the drinker, from the first flushing of the cheek, brightening of the eye, and unnatural mental excitement, to the general paralysis of complete drunkenness, belong equally to the poisonous effect of alcohol. Even the early phases of alcoholic disturbance, which are often improperly called "stimulating," are part and parcel of the injuriously disturbing influence of overdosage, and must be put in the same category with the more obviously poisonous effects of pronounced intoxication. Alcohol has thus a twofold action. First, it is capable, in proper doses, of being consumed and utilized as a force-producer; in which case there is no visible disturbance of normal function. Such action cannot be distinguished, either by the drinker or the physiologist, from that of a quickly digestible fluid food, and is no more an "excitement" or "stimulation," followed by a "recoil" or "depression," than is the action of a bowl of hot soup or a glass of milk. The second action is the poisonous influence of an excess of alcohol circulating in the

blood, which makes itself sensible to the drinker by
peculiar sensations and disturbances, and is not only
followed by " depression," but is itself a form of depression, — that is, a disturbance of balance; an
unnatural perturbation of the normal working of
the functions.'

" Abstinents are very fond of quoting the fact that
alcohol may be found in the brain of a person who
has died from excessive drinking; but, as Dr. Hammond pertinently says: ' The amount of essential oil
present in onions is far less in proportion than the
quantity of alcohol contained in the mildest wines;
and yet we cannot eat an onion without this oil
passing into the blood, and impregnating the air
expired in respiration with its peculiar odor.   Doubtless the brain of a person who has dined heartily on
onions would exhale the characteristic odor of the
vegetable.'

" Chronic alcoholic intoxication would rarely, if
ever, ensue from the moderate use of pure light
wines or malt liquors.   But it is impossible to get
pure wine.   It is not generally known that all the
foreign wines sold in this country are made stronger
by the addition of alcohol, before or after importa-
tion, to suit the strong taste of the American market.
Some of the choicest wines, when pure, do not contain more than six to ten per cent of alcohol, — no
more than good cider, — and no wine can, by fer-
mentation only, be made to contain more than
seventeen per cent of alcohol.   All over this is
added, even if there be no other adulteration.   And

the amount and quality of this adulteration is fearful. For details I must refer to the standard Toxicologys, such as Christison, Wetherbee, and others, and Hassall and others on the 'Adulterations of Food,' and to a summary in ' Alcohol, its Combinations, Adulterations, and Physical Effects,' by Col. Dudley, just published.

" If the so-called temperance party, instead of vainly attempting to prohibit the sale of liquors, regardless of what may be consumed outside of retail stores, would help to educate the people as to the adulterations now used in all wines, and would supply them with pure wine of the natural strength, with no alcohol added, they would accomplish more than they have yet accomplished in aiding the suppression of intemperance ; for the instinct to drink something stimulant exists, and will exist, and might as well be recognized. It is useless to ignore it or to attempt to destroy it. It exists in every people the world over."

The very delicate question whether alcohol is a food or a stimulant receives some light from the following statement of Dr. Bowditch. Professor Voit's authority in these matters is second to none : —

"ALCOHOL AS A NUTRITIVE AGENT.

" By H. P. Bowditch, M.D., Boston. Read before the Boston Society of Medical Sciences.

" The experiments of Dr. Subbotin [1] were performed on rabbits enclosed in an apparatus, by

---

[1] On the physiological importance of alcohol for the animal organism. Zeitschrift für Biologie, vii. 361.

means of which the exhalations of the skin and lungs could be examined for alcohol. The urine was also collected and examined for the same substance.

"The experiments showed that, in the first five hours after the introduction of 3.45 grammes of alcohol into the stomach of a rabbit, about 2 per cent was eliminated by the kidneys, and 5 per cent by the lungs and skin.

"Experiments extending over a greater length of time led to the conclusion that, usually, during twenty-four hours, at least 16 per cent of the injected alcohol leaves the body in an unchanged condition (or perhaps as aldehyde), and that besides this elimination by lungs, skin, and kidney, a portion of the alcohol is oxidized in the organism. Although by this oxidation force must be set free in the organism, the author does not consider that alcohol is on that account to be regarded as a nutriment, for the functions of the animal body depend for their performance, according to Dr. S., upon the transformation of living material, *i.e.*, of the constituent parts of the body, and not upon the decomposition of matter foreign to the body.

"In a note appended to Dr. Subbotin's essay, Professor Voit expresses himself as follows: 'I do not agree entirely with Dr. Subbotin in his views on the importance of alcohol as a nutriment. I define a nutriment as a substance which is capable of furnishing to the body any of its necessary constituents, or of preventing the removal of such constituents from the body. To the first class belong such substances as albumen (since it can be deposited as such in the body), or fat or water or the mineral constituents of the body; to the second class belong such substances as starch, which hinders the loss of fat from the body. If a nutriment is defined as a substance which, by decomposition, furnishes living force to the body, the definition would not be exhaustive, for it would exclude water and the mineral constituents of the body. Alcohol must, therefore, to a certain extent, be regarded as a nutriment, since, under its influence, fewer substances are decomposed in the body. It plays, in this respect, a similar (though quantitatively very different) part to that of starch, which also protects fat from decomposition, and, when taken in excess, causes deposition of fat in the organs or fatty degeneration. If a part of the alcohol is decomposed in the body into lower forms of chemical combination, it *must* give rise to living force, which either benefits the body in the form of heat, or may, perhaps, be used for the performance of mechanical work; the same is true of acetic acid, which is also not to be considered as an ultimate excretory product, and from which, therefore, in decomposition, potential force passes into living force.

"'It is another question, however, when we ask what importance alcohol has for us as a nutriment, and whether we take it in order to save fat from decomposition and furnish us with living force,— in other words, to introduce a nutriment into the

10

body. Since alcohol, when taken in considerable
amount, causes disturbances in the processes of the
animal economy, we cannot introduce it in quantities sufficient for nourishment as we do other nu-
triments, and in the amount which we can take
without injury its importance as a nutriment is too
small to be considered. In this point, then, I agree
entirely with Dr. Subbotin; we use alcohol not on
account of its importance as a nutriment, but on
account of its effects as a stimulant or relish.'

" Professor Voit's definition of a nutriment is rather
more comprehensive than those usually given; but
it has the merit of great exactness, and of leaving
no doubt as to its applicability to any given substance. Whether this definition or any other be
adopted, it is, of course, essential, as a preliminary
to the discussion of the nutritive value of alcohol or
any other substance, that we should define as exactly
as possible what we understand by the terms 'nutriment' and 'nutrition.'

" Although, as Professor Voit says, alcohol cannot, under normal circumstances, be introduced into
the body in sufficient amount to be of any importance as a nutriment without producing toxic effects,
may it not be that in those morbid conditions of the
system where large amounts of alcohol are borne
without causing narcotism, the nutritive properties
of the substance really become important, and that
patients who are supported by alcohol through peri-
ods of great weakness or exhaustion are really nour-
ished and not simply stimulated by it?"

We believe there is now no difference worth noticing from the opinion that, in proper doses, it is a useful agent. We cite Dr. Woodman, in the "London Medical Record," May 13, 1874: —

"Riegel on the Influence of Alcohol on Temperature of the Human Body: from Deutsches Archiv für Klinische Medicin. Riegel concludes that although alcohol scarcely deserves the reputation given to it in England, as a decided depressor of temperature, yet, on the other hand, it never essentially raises the temperature, — the constant dread of continental practitioners, — and it is decidedly one of those things which diminish bodily waste, like tea and coffee. On the whole, his experiments confirm those of Binz and Bouvier (we may add, of Dr. Parkes, Dogiel, Sydney Ringer — and the Reporter)."

Dr. Binz, of Bonn, as cited in "The American Journal of the Medical Sciences," January, 1874, p. 231, "said his experiments showed a threefold action, — the diminution of the heat of the body, reduction of the putrid processes, and raising of the action of the heart. Alcohol was more than a simple stimulant; it was a strong antipyretic, and an equally powerful antiseptic. It was *à priori* to be expected that alcohol would not be without its influence on the metamorphosis of tissues. An agent that, consumed in large doses, clearly lowered the combustion, must also be supposed to decrease the urea and the carbonic acid; and this was in reality the case."

Another opinion of alcohol is, that it is "an unstable combination of carbon, hydrogen, and oxygen, which,

when undergoing decomposition, is capable of setting
free a large amount of force (*e.g.*, when burning in
a spirit-lamp). If this decomposition takes place in
the body, as it doubtless does to a considerable
extent, the force set free must take the form of heat
or muscular work. In other words, alcohol must
contribute to the maintenance of the animal economy
in the same way that food does. The nutritive
power of alcohol is, however, in normal conditions of
the body, very slight, for the reason pointed out by
Prof. Voit. But when we see a patient suffering from an
exhausting disease, actually living weeks and months
on little else than a daily bottle of wine, we are
forced to the conclusion that the toxic influence of
alcohol in the nervous system is for some reason held
in abeyance, so that the nutritive power becomes of
importance, and that the patient is really *fed*, and not
merely *stimulated*, by wine."

Dr. Anstie, in the " Practitioner," July, 1874 : " It is
scarcely possible, therefore, but that the solution of
the questions as to the action of alcohol in the body
will also bring about the discovery of new physiological facts of great interest and importance : —

" 1. If alcohol be a force-producing food, as seems
by far the most likely, it is probably of great value
in that capacity, on account of the rapidity with
which its transformations take place. It is, however,
abundantly certain, that beyond a certain dosage
(which is pretty clearly made out for the average,
though of course there are individual exceptions in
both directions) it becomes a narcotic poison of a

very dangerous character in every respect, not the least disadvantage being that it cannot be eliminated to any considerable extent.

" 2. If alcohol does not disappear by oxidation, it must undergo some as yet quite unknown transformation, after which it must escape unrecognized in the excretions. I have heard various attempts to suggest such modes of disappearance, but nothing, so far, which wears any air of probability.

" 3. If alcohol, however, be indeed oxidized, and yet does not beget force which can be used in the organism, this would be the strangest possible discovery. Considering the very high theoretical force-value of the 600 to 800 grains of absolute alcohol which millions of sober persons are taking every day, we may well be hopeless of any reasonable answer to the question, Why does not this large development of wholly useless force within the body produce some violent symptoms of disturbance ? "

The effects produced on the brain by alcohol are much exaggerated in the estimation of the public. " *P. Ruge*, on the effect of alcohol upon the animal organism, quoted from Virchow's *Archiv, XLIX.,* in Rosenthal's ' Centralblat,' 1870. The author desired to investigate the anatomical changes of animal organs produced by alcoholism, and experimented on twenty-two grown dogs and five rabbits. They finally got as much as 100 ccm. of 90 per cent alcohol daily, and that for months. Upon comparing his results with the Charité Hospital reports of Berlin for 1867 and 1868, he did not find any different results as to the effect of alcohol upon the human brain. Of ten persons who died of delirium tremens, but one showed a decided hemorrhagic pachymeningitis, one an increase of the dura, and in the rest the texture of the brain was normal. On the other hand, fortyseven cases of pachymeningitis were caused without any abuse of spirits. The five rabbits did not show any material change of any organ. Former observations of alcoholic influence upon the animal temperature were corroborated. The temperature of dogs, especially when they were intoxicated, sank by several degrees; their pulse and respiration increased at the same time."

"Pavey on Food and Dietetics"—the latest authority in these matters—says: "It will be seen that much divergence of opinion has prevailed upon the prime question, whether alcohol is to be regarded as possessing any alimentary value or not. It will suffice here to refer the reader to what has been already mentioned, and to state that the weight of evidence appears to be in favor of the affirmative. A small portion seems, undoubtedly, to escape from the body unconsumed; but there is reason to believe that the larger portion is retained and turned to account in the system."   p. 357.

"Beer is a refreshing, exhilarating, nutritive, and, when taken in excess, an intoxicating beverage." p. 365.

"Although chemistry displays the existence of a number of constituents in wine, yet it may be considered that in its action upon the system we have not to deal with the effect of its independent principles, but with a liquid in which the ingredients should be so amalgamated, incorporated, or blended together as to make a homogeneous whole. For instance, if we look to alcohol, which forms the most active component, the effects of a certain amount of this principle, as it is contained in wine, are not identical with those of the same amount diluted to an equal extent with water. The alcohol appears to become blended with the other ingredients, and, in this state, to exert a somewhat modified action upon the system." p. 376.

We may add that Dr. Pavey does not say whether it is wise or unwise to take alcoholic drinks. He leaves the matter to each individual. We hold that legislators should be equally discreet.

Cambridge : Press of John Wilson & Son.

LAOCOON. An Essay upon the Limits of Painting and Poetry. With remarks illustrative of various points in the History of Ancient Art. By GOTTHOLD EPHRAIM LESSING. Translated by ELLEN FROTHINGHAM. 16mo. Price $1.50.

In reference to this work, we can give our readers no better proof of its merit than by quoting the words of an English critic uttered many years ago : "The author of the ' Laocoon ' was perhaps the greatest critic of modern times. The object of this celebrated work is to show that the isolation of the several fine arts from each other is essential to their perfection, and that their common aim is the production of beauty. The peculiar province of poetry is proved to be entirely distinct both from that of morality and of philosophy ; being limited, strictly speaking, to the exhibition of ideal actions. These views, in which Lessing differed widely from Klopstock, who made moral beauty, and also from Wieland, who considered nature and truth, as the great aim of poetry, but in which he agreed with Aristotle, and was closely followed in their æsthetical theories by Goethe, Schiller, and Humboldt, were enforced with great argumentative power, extraordinary purity and correctness of taste, and with rich and pertinent illustrations from the art and literature of Greece."

From the Boston Transcript.

It is a matter for real congratulation that Messrs. Roberts Brothers have given us the "Laocoon" of Lessing in a form accessible to readers ignorant of German. Miss Frothingham has evidently done her work of translation as a labor of love. Her rendering is at once accurate, and in pure, flowing English ; an achievement very difficult to accomplish where the whole grammatical structure of two languages differs so widely. It is also a feature of great value toward the general usefulness of the book that she has appended translations of the many passages from Latin and Greek authors through which Lessing illustrates his argument.

The growing interest in our country in questions of art and criticism ought to secure for this work a wide class of readers. No thoughtful person ever forgets the outburst of enthusiasm its first reading awakened in him. Even Goethe said of it that in the confused period of his own youth it cleared up the whole heavens to him and made his path plain before him. As an offset to such books as those of Ruskin, marvellously rich and suggestive, but full of subjective caprice and dogmatism, it teaches invaluable lessons of method. Lessing was a legislator in the domain of criticism. His insight was so nearly unerring, and his knowledge so vast and accurate, that his verdicts stand like those of a Mansfield or Marshall in the courts of law.

. . . The book must be read and re-read. It created an epoch in art criticism when it first appeared, and its lessons are as fresh and weighty to-day as ever. On every page great principles are developed which help one to an ever deeper appreciation of the works of the great masters in art and literature.

———

ENGLISH LESSONS FOR ENGLISH PEOPLE.

By Rev. E. A. ABBOTT, M.A., and Prof. J. R. SEELEY, M.A. Part I. — Vocabulary. Part II. — Diction. Part III. — Metre. Part IV. — Hints on Selection and Arrangement. Appendix. 16mo. Price $1.50.

From the London Athenæum.

The object of this book is evidently a practical one. It is intended for ordinary use by a large circle of readers; and though designed principally for boys, may be read with advantage by many of more advanced years. One of the lessons which it professes to teach, "to use the right word in the right place," is one which no one should despise. The accomplishment is a rare one, and many of the hints here given are truly admirable.

From the Southern Review.

The study of Language can never be exhausted. Every time it is looked at by a man of real ability and culture, some new phase starts into view. The origin of Language; its relations to the mind; its history; its laws; its development; its struggles; its triumphs; its devices; its puzzles; its ethics, — every thing about it is full of interest.

Here is a delightful book, by two men of recognized authority, — the head Master of London School, and the Professor of Modern History in the University of Cambridge, the notable author of "Ecce Homo." The book is so comprehensive in its scope that it seems almost miscellaneous. It treats of the vocabulary of the English Language; Diction as appropriate to this or that sort of composition; selection and arguments of topics; Metre, and an Appendix on Logic. All this in less than three hundred pages. Within this space so many subjects cannot be treated exhaustively; and no one is, unless we may except Metre, to which about eighty pages are devoted, and about which all seems to be said that is worth saying, — possibly more. But on each topic some of the best things are said in a very stimulating way. The student will desire to study more thoroughly the subject into which such pleasant openings are here given; and the best prepared teacher will be thankful for the number of striking illustrations gathered up to his hand.

The abundance and freshness of the quotations makes the volume very attractive reading, without reference to its didactic value.

Sold by all booksellers. Mailed, postpaid, by the Publishers,

ROBERTS BROTHERS, BOSTON.

THE
INTELLECTUAL LIFE.

By PHILIP GILBERT HAMERTON,

AUTHOR OF

"A Painter's Camp," "Thoughts About Art," "The Unknown River," "Chapters on Animals."

Square 12mo, cloth, gilt. Price $2.00.

From the Christian Union.

"In many respects this is a remarkable book, — the last and best production of a singularly well balanced and finely cultured mind. No man whose life was not lifted above the anxieties of a bread-winning life could have written this work; which is steeped in that sweetness and light, the virtues of which Mr. Arnold so eloquently preaches. Compared with Mr. Hamerton's former writings, 'The Intellectual Life' is incomparably his best production. . . . . But above all, and specially as critics, are we charmed with the large impartiality of the writer. Mr Hamerton is one of those peculiarly fortunate men who have the inclination and means to live an ideal life. From his youth he has lived in an atmosphere of culture and light, moving with clipped wings in a charmed circle of thought. Possessing a peculiarly refined and delicate nature, a passionate love of beauty, and purity and art; and having the means to gratify his tastes, Mr. Hamerton has held himself aloof from the commonplace routine of life; and by constant study of books and nature and his fellow men, has so purified his intellect and tempered his judgment, that he is able to view things from a higher platform even than more able men whose natures have been soured, cramped, or influenced by the necessities of a laborious existence. Hence the rare impartiality of his decisions, the catholicity of his views, and the sympathy with which he can discuss the most irreconcilable doctrines. To read Mr. Hamerton's writings is an intellectual luxury. They are not boisterously strong, or exciting, or even very forcible; but they are instinct with the finest feeling, the broadest sympathies, and a philosophic calm that acts like an opiate on the unstrung nerves of the hard-wrought literary reader. Calm, equable, and beautiful, 'The Intellectual Life,' when contrasted with the sensational and half digested clap-trap that forms so large a portion of contemporary literature, reminds one of the old picture of the nuns, moving about, calm and self-possessed, through the fighting and blaspheming crowds that thronged the beleagured city."

"This book is written with perfect singleness of purpose to help others towards an intellectual life," says the *Boston Daily Advertiser.*

"It is eminently a book of counsel and instruction," says the *Boston Post.*

"A book, which it seems to us will take a permanent place in literature, says the *New York Daily Mail.*

Sold by all Booksellers.   Mailed, postpaid, by the Publishers,

ROBERTS BROTHERS, Boston.

GOETHE'S

HERMANN AND DOROTHEA.

TRANSLATED FROM THE GERMAN

By ELLEN FROTHINGHAM.

WITH ILLUSTRATIONS.

Thin 8vo, cloth, gilt, bevelled boards. Price $2.00.
A cheaper edition, 16mo, *cloth. Price* $1.00.

"Miss Frothingham's translation is something to be glad of: it lends itself kindly to perusal, and it presents Goethe's charming poem in the metre of the original. . . . It is not a poem which could be profitably used in an argument for the enlargement of the sphere of woman : it teaches her subjection, indeed, from the lips of a beautiful girl, which are always so fatally convincing ; but it has its charm, nevertheless, and will serve at least for an agreeable picture of an age when the ideal woman was a creature around which grew the beauty and comfort and security of home." — *Atlantic Monthly.*

"The poem itself is bewitching. Of the same metre as Longfellow's ' Evangeline,' its sweet and measured cadences carry the reader onward with a real pleasure as he becomes more and more absorbed in this descriptive wooing song. It is a sweet volume to read aloud in a select circle of intelligent friends." — *Providence Press.*

"Miss Frothingham has done a good service, and done it well, in translating this famous idyl, which has been justly called ' one of the most faultless poems of modern times.' Nothing can surpass the simplicity, tenderness, and grace of the original, and these have been well preserved in Miss Frothingham's version. Her success is worthy of the highest praise, and the mere English reader can scarcely fail to read the poem with the same delight with which it has always been read by those familiar with the German. Its charming pictures of domestic life, the strength and delicacy of its characterization, the purity of tone and ardent love of country which breathe through it, must always make it one of the most admired of Goethe's works." — *Boston Christian Register.*

Sold everywhere. Mailed, postpaid, by the Publishers,

ROBERTS BROTHERS, Boston.